D1523072

Nintendo Magic
Winning the Videogame Wars

By Osamu Inoue

Translated by Paul Tuttle Starr

VERTICAL.

Originally published in Japanese as *Nintendou: "Odoroki" o umu houteishiki*
by Nihon Keizai Shinbun Shuppansha, Tokyo, 2009.

ISBN 978-1-934287-22-4

Manufactured in the United States of America

First Edition

Vertical, Inc.
1185 Avenue of the Americas 32nd Floor
New York, NY 10036
www.vertical-inc.com

TABLE OF CONTENTS

In September of 2008, the world plunged into a once-in-a-century financial storm sparked by the surprise bankruptcy of Lehman Brothers Holdings.

Goods went unsold. Inventory and production costs inflated, causing production itself to fall. Reorganization of manufacturing bases forced accelerated layoffs, and the cost of that reorganization in turn impacted profits. Exchange-rate losses mounted on a strengthening yen.

Pandemonium doubled and redoubled. Between January and February of 2009, it became clear that a massive number of Japanese firms would see their profits disappear.

Toyota, Nissan, Panasonic, Hitachi, Toshiba, Sony—in an avalanche, the performance forecasts for all the major players toppled into the red to the tune of hundreds of billions of yen. The losses of the top ten electronics companies alone passed the two *trillion* yen mark. That winter, at the edge of a seemingly bottomless recession, they all felt the chill of the century.

Except Nintendo.

It had been six years and ten months since Satoru Iwata had taken the helm of Nintendo as president. March of 2009 became a memorable month for the company. Their portable game system, the Nintendo DS, had sold one hundred million units around the world, while the home console game system, the Wii, broke the fifty million unit mark.

The hundred million DS units sold in the four years and three months since its introduction were a record in the home videogame industry. Likewise, the Wii had only taken two years and five months to sell fifty million units, coming under the previous record of a little less than three years, which had been held by Sony's PlayStation 2 (PS2) system.

Nintendo was both trailblazer and king of the videogame industry.

They had grown into an international brand that could stand shoulder-to-shoulder with the likes of Toyota, and was fast establishing a reputation for innovation that put it in a league with companies like Apple and Google. Its growing performance also suited such comparisons.

Sales for the fiscal year ending in March 2008 were 3.3 times what they had been the first year of the Iwata era (period ending March 2003)—coming to 1.6724 trillion yen, with the operating profits from their core business likewise 4.9 times higher, at 487.2 billion yen.

That amounted to sales of 440 million yen and operating profits of 130 million yen for each of the roughly 3,800 people Nintendo employed on a consolidated basis. Calculated against the number of core employees, responsible for most of that revenue, those numbers rise to 1.1 billion yen and 330 million yen, respectively.

In Toyota's case, with its seventy thousand-strong core workforce, sales per employee were 380 million yen, with operating profits of 33 million yen per. Nintendo's far superior revenue and productivity is all the more stunning in that it not only weathered the panicked stampede that was the worldwide economic crisis of late 2008 but achieved growth despite it.

For the fiscal year ending in March 2009, Nintendo estimates record sales of 1.82 trillion yen. Operating profits, too, will reach a record high of 530 billion yen, putting them above Toyota, at the very top of Japanese industry.

Entering January, the company adjusted their performance forecasts for the 2009 fiscal year downward—but unlike other companies, this was due only to the strong yen. The changing exchange rates took their toll on Nintendo, which exported 85% of its products, forcing them to lower forecasts for sales and operating profits by 180 billion yen and 120 billion yen, respectively, with net profits also expected to be down by 180 billion yen.

But that was all; in North America, the crisis' source, their business was exploding.

"In 2008, we sold 10.17 million Wii systems, and 9.95 million

Nintendo DS systems. Both of these are records for gaming system sales over a single year," Iwata proudly stated at a financial results briefing held in January 2009.

The credit crisis and consumer recession seemed irrelevant. *Wii Fit*—a piece of fitness software for the Wii—flew off shelves when packaged in a set with the Wii system itself.

Sales of the Wii system boomed; in North America between October and December of 2008, they were up 54% compared with the same quarter a year earlier. In Europe (also includes some regions outside of Japan and North America), sales were up 91%. Surprisingly, sales of the DS also continued to grow, fully five holiday seasons after its initial release—they were up 4% over the previous year in North America, and up 11% in Europe.

Even with the end of the 2008 holiday season and the specter of consumer recession looming over early 2009, Nintendo's success continued.

According to the NPD Group, an American research firm, in January 2009 the American videogame market (including hardware and software) had grown 13% relative to the previous year, and most of that growth had come from Nintendo products. The hardware leader was the Wii, at 680,000 units, followed by the DS at 510,000. The top three software titles were all Wii games, with Wii Fit selling 780,000 copies, breaking the record for January game sales.

Newspapers ran headlines like "Recession-proof Videogames" or "Boosted by Nesting Instinct Purchase Trends," but ascribing Nintendo's success during the recession to the fact that it was in the videogame business is a mistake.

In reality, rival Sony's console sales had fallen. During the last quarter of 2008, sales of its home game system, the Playstation 3 (PS3), were down 9% from the same quarter a year previous, with Playstation Portable (PSP) sales down 12%. January 2009 console sales were still down from the previous year.

Masashi Morita, an analyst with Okasan Securities who's familiar with the videogame industry, put it thus: "It's not that Nintendo was strong in a recession—it would be more accurate to say that the recession is irrelevant to them. The reason being that even in a strong economy, boring products don't sell."

Indeed, Nintendo had brushed aside the implosion of the century, achieving nothing less than a triumph that would go down in both company and economic history.

But what is the source of this miraculous success? And what is the strength unique to Nintendo that has enabled such success? Surprisingly few people are able to answer those questions.

With Nintendo performing so spectacularly on the world stage, the media worldwide is eager to know their secret. But nearly all have been turned away at the door. That's just the way the company is.

Nintendo prefers not to have its management discussed by outsiders, even eschewing praise. As a result, despite the company's success, opportunities for individual interviews are extremely rare, and there are essentially no publications that deal with Nintendo's management.

We'll talk about our products as much as you like. But a profile of the company president, or a discussion of our management practices and ideals? Those have nothing to do with products. Our attention is focused on game hardware and software. We hold thorough investor meetings. There's no point in doing individual interviews. Anytime we have something to say, we'll put it on our website.

This would sum up Nintendo's approach to PR, and it's an attitude that's only become entrenched as they've grown to compete with the world's giants.

To borrow Iwata's own words, "We've had our ideas copied so often that we've gotten really sensitive about it." Nintendo's reluctance to discuss its management can be seen as the proof of how serious the company is about protecting itself from competitors.

At the root of that corporate culture is the assumption that even if they were to discuss their management, outsiders wouldn't understand—an eminently Nintendo-like notion. Thus, not seeing any point in such discourses, they practice rigorous information control, consistently keeping exposure to the minimum possible.

However, *Nikkei Business*, my employer, was given the chance to interview, at length, Nintendo miracle-workers like Satoru Iwata and Shigeru Miyamoto, and was fortunate enough to have the pleasure of speaking with Hiroshi Yamauchi, former president of and current advisor to the company. This is the first time he's spoken openly about the management of Nintendo since retiring.

The result of these interviews was a special series of articles than ran in *Nikkei Business*. Considerable insight into Nintendo's unique management style seeped out from around the edges of these executives' words, but the constraints of the magazine format limited what could see print. For much of the material to remain unpublished, particularly in these dark and worsening times for the Japanese economy, would have been a shame. Now more than ever, Nintendo's steady advancement makes it an invaluable exemplar of Japanese enterprise.

"Only The Paranoid Survive," Intel co-founder Andy Grove has famously said. "When it comes to business, I believe in the value of paranoia."

Meanwhile, when Apple co-founder and CEO Steve Jobs gave a commencement speech at Stanford University, he left the graduates with the words "Stay hungry, stay foolish."

There's a whiff of these ideas about Nintendo, but only a whiff. At a glance it's reminiscent of an energetic Silicon Valley enterprise—but Nintendo's headquarters are in Kyoto, the old capital of Japan, and the company has 120 years of history. Its culture is clearly not that of a Silicon Valley startup.

What is Nintendo's philosophy? And where does it come from?

We cannot help but probe again the formula of Nintendo's success: whatever it may be that lies behind their weathering of the shifting trends that buffet the entertainment industry, whatever it is that has turned them into a world-renowned case of business excellence.

That special quality is relevant not just in the videogame or software worlds, but for any company seeking the breakthrough that will put them above the waves of homogenization and price wars.

The positions and relationships of all persons appearing in this book were current as of April 2009. The author hopes you will forgive his omission of honorifics.

Osamu Inoue
April 2009

1

Crisis on the Horizon

"The result of all our hard work on making wonderful games was that people without the time and energy to devote to them were just saying 'heck with it' and walking away. The more we investigated this, the more severe we realized the problem was."

—Iwata

The Challenge of the DS: One System Per Person

On the afternoon of October 2, 2008, over a thousand journalists and videogame industry workers gathered at the main gymnasium of Yoyogi Park in the Harajuku district of Tokyo. Invitations were being rigorously checked, and there was a line to enter the venue. Once the temporary seating that had been set up within the arena was filled to capacity, there was a moment of silence before Satoru Iwata, president of Nintendo, emerged on the stage to loud music and flashy lights.

Thunderous applause echoed through the venue, calling to mind one of Apple CEO Steve Jobs's famous keynote addresses. Iwata was surely the only executive in Japan suited to such a performance. After a brief introduction, he got down to business.

"On December 2, 2004, Nintendo introduced the original Nintendo DS, as part of our basic strategy to grow the gaming population. It's been exactly three years and ten months since then, and today I'd like to introduce the newest member of the DS family, the Nintendo DSi," said Iwata, holding the new camera-equipped, music-playing DS model high.

The DS had already sold 23 million units in Japan, and it was clear Iwata expected to sell many, many more.

The system had sold astonishingly well worldwide. The DS—which first went on sale in the United States in November 2004, coming to Japan a month later—had by December 2008 reached 96.22 million units globally.

Nearly four years after its initial release, it was still going strong, and in March of 2009 it broke the 100 million unit barrier in record time, faster than any game system before it.

Up until that point, only three systems had ever sold 100 million units. Sony Computer Entertainment's (SCE) first home system, the PlayStation, took nine and a half years to do it; its successor, the PlayStation 2 (PS2) needed five years, nine months. The only portable system to achieve the feat was Nintendo's own Game Boy, which—along with the puzzle game *Tetris*—took the world by storm following its 1989 introduction, but it took 11 years to pass the 100 million mark. The DS's explosive popularity put them all to shame.

It's common knowledge that unlike its portable predecessors, the DS was equipped with unconventional features like twin displays, stylus input, and speech recognition. It featured intuitive controls, where players could watch the top screen while using the stylus on the bottom screen and speaking into the microphone. The name "DS" was derived from the double screens of the unit.

Defying the industry's common sense of a single display and button controls and proliferating at an unprecedented rate, the DS eludes conventional wisdom.

One standard outlook in the videogame industry is of a "five-year-generation cycle" of first selling a wave of consoles, then building a business based on game sales. But the DS had stamina that put it in another class—and despite nearly surpassing adoption capacity in Japan, Nintendo was aiming still higher.

Success, though, had come gradually to the DS. Sales had started slower than its predecessor, the Game Boy Advance.

Within Japan, the DS whirlwind really only started to blow almost exactly a year after its introduction, during the year-end sales of 2005. At major retailers, lines of people waiting for the system became daily occurrences, and supplies were constantly low. The DS attracted young and old, male and female alike, and the media coverage of the phenomenon was unrelenting.

In March 2006, right in the midst of the craze, Nintendo introduced the DS Lite. It was smaller in every dimension than the original DS, and weighed about 20% less. The release of the new device threw gasoline on the fire of the system's blazing popularity.

Starting in April 2006, Japanese sales of the DS hit 9.12 million, just shy of an even 10 million. It was a landmark and a record for game system sales over a single year.

The next year, sales had fallen to 6.36 million, and entering 2008

Unit Sales Comparison: DS and Game Boy

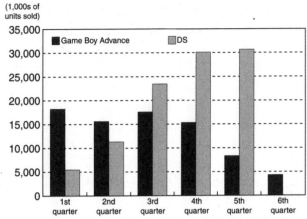

Note: Global total. DS 5th quarter an estimate, 31.5 million units forecast by May 7 settling.
Source: Nintendo

it was clear that the abnormal adoption rate of the DS was slowing. It was hardly surprising; by the end of 2008 over 25 million units had been sold in Japan.

A simple calculation revealed one DS for every five people in Japan. According to the conventional wisdom of the videogame world, the DS would start to slow down as people quietly waited for the next generation of portable videogame systems. But now Iwata was claiming that the DS era was far from over.

"I'm sure there are a lot of people who would decide that with 20 million units out there, the market is saturated. But we think that if we can show people some new ways a portable game system can fit into their lifestyle, there's still potential for growth in the platform."

The DSi was a proposal to breathe new life into the platform, fully four years after the introduction of the original DS. The length, width, and weight of the device were roughly the same as the original DS, but it was 12% thinner, and the LCD displays were both brighter and bigger—3.25 inches, as opposed to the previous three inches.

But there were other improvements—the DSi had a camera, and could play music files. The aim was not to compete with cell phones

that had the same capabilities, but rather to encourage users to play
with sound and pictures. It was just the sort of idea you'd expect from
Nintendo. The DSi let users decorate photographs like they would
using a print club machine, warp images with the stylus, even mash
together their own faces with a friend's. The music player likewise let
users change the speed and pitch of both music loaded onto the unit
and sounds recorded with the built-in microphone.

With these added features, Nintendo and the DS aimed to strike
into unexplored territory: the realm of one system per person.

"Even in households that already have a DS, we'd like to create
a trend that shifts away from having one DS shared among multiple
family members—so instead of one unit per household, one per
person."

Iwata's reasoning led to the "i" in the new DS's name. According
to Nintendo's research, an average of 2.8 people per household used
the DS, but the average number of units per household was 1.8. They
wanted to give everyone their own DS, closing this gap—and the DSi
was their plan to pull it off.

So far, Iwata's strategy is working. At the end of the fiscal year ending
March 2009—the fifth since the platform's introduction—Nintendo
equaled its record performance from the year before, selling 30 million
units worldwide. The DS whirlwind had crossed the oceans; more
DSs were sold in North America and Europe than Japan. The DSi will
only increase the platform's longevity.

Okasan Securities, a firm respected for its videogame industry
analysis, projects that by March 2011, DS sales will reach 150 million
units. When that happens, it will surpass Sony's PS2 home system
(which sold 130 million units) to become the bestselling videogame
system ever created.

The DS's success is unprecedented in the history of videogames,
and the achievements of its unconventional hardware design are
significant. But you can't talk about the DS whirlwind without
discussing the DS's software—with its new genres that flew in the
face of existing ideas about games.

The President's *Brain Age*

He headed for the airport, putting the clamor behind him.

"We will begin selling at 6:55. Please form a line here! Again, purchases will be limited to one unit per customer!"

It was 6 AM on December 2, 2004. Commuters were still thin on the ground at the early hour, but there was a line of people stretching out the door of the Big Camera electronics store in the Yurakucho district of Tokyo. It was the launch date for the Nintendo DS. Big Camera, Yodobashi Camera, and every other major electronics retailer would be opening early for the occasion.

You would think that as president of the company, Iwata would be on hand for the launch of the long-awaited next-generation system, but he was nowhere to be found. And no wonder—for he was even then heading for Tohoku University, in the city of Sendai, in northern Miyagi prefecture, to light the fuse on what would become an explosive hit for the new platform.

No wo Kitaeru Otona no DS Torehningu—or as it's known in English, *Brain Age: Train Your Brain in Minutes a Day!* is famous for its contribution to the perfect storm that was the DS. As of December 2008, the *Brain Age* series has sold over 30 million copies worldwide, a standout title even within the successful DS catalog.

Brain Age includes over ten minigames, including "Calculations x 20," where the player must write out the answers to twenty simple arithmetic problems, "Low to High," where the player must quickly memorize the positions of numerals displayed on the screen, then touch those places in ascending order, and "Reading Aloud," in which the player must quickly read aloud from an excerpt of a classic work of literature. It was the first game Iwata had produced since taking the helm of Nintendo.

It was a pair of bestselling books that he found in a bookstore that were the trigger—*No wo Kitaeru Otona no Keisan Doriru* and *No wo Kitaeru Otona no Onyomi Doriru* (the former was published in English as *Train Your Brain: 60 Days to a Better Brain*). The books originated from a collaboration between Professor Ryuta Kawashima of Tohoku University—a neuroscientist who studied the cerebral activity of patients recovering from injuries to their cognitive ability—and the Kumon franchise of tutoring centers, originators of the famous Kumon Method of arithmetic education. Based on Professor Kawashima's research, which concluded that doing simple math and reading exercises was effective for stimulating neural activity, the books included a course of 50 to 100 problems a day, five days a week, for 12 weeks. Word-of-mouth alone made the books a rare hit, and they had sold 1.2 million copies nationwide by June 2004.

Iwata took note of this success and immediately contacted Professor Kawashima, and by the summer of 2004 the *Brain Age* project was underway. The first prototype of the software reached Iwata in September of 2004, just two months before the DS's launch. For his part, Iwata was satisfied by its progress.

"I want to see Professor Kawashima's reaction with my own eyes. I'll fly out to see him as soon as I can."

Iwata wasted no time in getting Kawashima to agree to another meeting. But they were both busy men. By sheer coincidence, the first free day that the two had in common was the launch date for the DS.

Nonetheless, Iwata did not hesitate to head for Sendai and Professor Kawashima on December 2—launch day for the hardware that would decide Nintendo's future. He was entirely aware that by all rights, on a day like this, the head of the company should either be out and visible in public, or holed up in the headquarters, ready for emergencies.

Ten days after the DS launch, SCE president Ken Kutaragi would make a public display of handing the first PlayStation Portable (PSP) units to fans lined up at the Shinjuku Yodobashi Camera and Shibuya Tsutaya electronics retailers.

But as far as Iwata was concerned, finishing *Brain Age* was far more important that showing his face at the DS launch. His meeting with Kawashima was scheduled for 30 minutes, but in the end it went to three hours.

"There's nobody at the company that blames me for going to

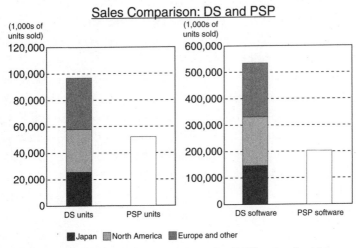

Sales Comparison: DS and PSP

Legend: ■ Japan ▨ North America ▨ Europe and other

Note: Total up to year-end 2008. DS numbers represent units sold; PSP numbers, the global total of units shipped by March 2006 and sold thereafter.

Sendai," says Iwata, explaining his enthusiasm for the project. He was dead on target—*Brain Age* became the impetus behind the DS's continuing growth in Japan, giving both adults who had given up on videogames and those who'd never been interested in them to begin with a reason to buy a DS.

The system had shown decent progress in the marketplace, but the majority of early DS buyers were videogame fans and elementary and middle school students. By the end of March 2005, four months after the launch, it had sold 2 million units—hardly earth-shattering. But with the release of *Brain Age* a month later, things were about to turn around.

The first week after its release, *Brain Age* sold 50,000 copies. It continued to move a few tens of thousands of copies a week, and heading into summer, instead of slowing, sales began to pick up, thanks to office workers in their 20s and 30s buying the game during the August holidays.

Brain Age was able to track the performance of up to four players. "Hey, Mom, let's see how old your brain is! C'mon, try it!" The game was proving invaluable as a reason for families to huddle together.

Children were turning into DS ambassadors to their middle-aged parents, giving them the opportunity to experience videogames. As the phenomenon spread, those same parents were going on to buy DS units and copies of *Brain Age*.

That September saw something unprecedented in videogame history. The week of Respect-for-the-Aged day (September 15), *Brain Age* sales suddenly broke their first-week sales record. Nintendo found that people were buying the game—which was now talked about as being useful for preventing cognitive degeneration—as a gift for elderly relatives, along with a DS to play it on.

Just like the *Otona* ("Adult") in its Japanese title suggested, the game was penetrating an older demographic, and by November 2005, six months after its launch, it passed 700,000 copies sold, going on to break a million in the end-of-year sales rush and causing the DS to sell out in various parts of the nation. The release of the sequel in December of that year only accelerated the march. Both the original and the sequel have since gone on to sell over 5 million copies in Japan, totaling 11 million for the series—a huge hit.

Nintendo worked to expand the videogame market by supporting games like this—titles which appealed to adults who'd either forgotten about videogames or who'd never cared in the first place. Having gone to the trouble of picking up their first portable game system in years—and often their first *ever*—they would wind up buying the games they'd played in their youth (the *Super Mario* series, for example), which boosted the game market as a whole. According to Nintendo's research, among DS users whose first game was *Brain Age*, 35% went on to buy another game within 90 days, and 10% bought at least 11 games.

This trend was the direct result of the plan to grow the gaming population that Iwata had pursued ever since becoming president, and *Brain Age* was a key component of that plan.

Brain Age bore that burden admirably—not just in Japan, but abroad as well.

However, there were other games that contributed to the DS's overseas success. Another killer app designed to appeal to non-gaming adults was *Nintendogs*.

Nintendogs—which launched in Japan in April 2005, hitting overseas markets in August and September of the same year—let users care for a virtual puppy, using stylus input on the touch screen as well as speech recognition via the DS's microphone. Users could call the dog's name, feed it, take it for walks—even toss a frisbee around for it to catch. Those seemingly banal activities were the entire point of the game.

You could barely call it a game, and yet, by the end of 2006, *Nintendogs* sold 4 million copies each in Europe and North America. Overseas growth continued into 2007, and by December 2008 worldwide sales reached 21.67 million copies, of which more than 90% were outside Japan.

Having developed both an intuitive game system and software that anybody could approach, Nintendo had recaptured people who were drifting away from videogames across the world. The lessons of the DS would be passed on to the home console that followed it.

The Wii and the Fight to Grow the Gaming Population
It was Microsoft that touched off the three-way battle for control of the gaming industry.

But did anyone then imagine how things would turn out—with housewives, physical therapy patients, and the British royal family alike all pointing a certain white controller at their TV screens?

In November 2005, when Microsoft unveiled the Xbox 360 and in doing so ushered in the next generation of videogame systems, most analysts with experience in the game industry predicted that Sony's PlayStation 3 would cruise to easy victory.

It could play High Definition Blu-Ray discs, and came equipped with a supercomputer-like "Cell" processor. The two technologies interfaced to create astounding graphics, which would—the received wisdom went—capture the hearts of videogame fans.

Of the three next-gen systems, Nintendo's Wii was the only one

Next-Generation Home Console Shares

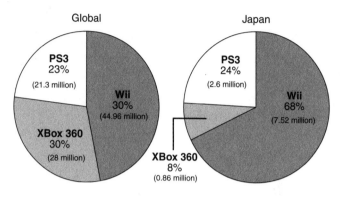

Global

PS3
23%
(21.3 million)

Wii
30%
(44.96 million)

XBox 360
30%
(28 million)

XBox 360
8%
(0.86 million)

Japan

PS3
24%
(2.6 million)

Wii
68%
(7.52 million)

Note: Total up to year-end 2008.

unable to display High Definition (HD) graphics, so the industry analysts that favored it for success were few and far between.

But with the battle underway, it was the Wii that took the lead. The Wii—which launched in late 2006, a year after the Xbox 360—surpassed the Microsoft system in the blink of an eye, extending its lead at twice the adoption pace of the PS3.

Nintendo's rivals were forces to be reckoned with.

While Nintendo had created the modern videogame industry with their Family Computer (or Nintendo Entertainment System, as it was known in the US) in 1983, starting in the mid-1990s they'd taken a vicious beating at the hands of Sony.

SCE—a subsidiary of Sony—released the first PlayStation in 1994, followed by the PS2 in 2000, and the two consoles had utterly dominated the marketplace. To follow that success, Sony had invested over 200 billion yen along with the will and pride that came with being the leader of the electronics industry into creating the PS3.

On the other hand, there was Microsoft, which had hurled itself headlong into the videogame market. The company lacked experience but had vast reserves of capital exceeding even Sony's. In June of 2002, realizing that their Xbox console (which competed with the PS2) was falling behind, they summarily decided to invest two billion dollars over five years to developing their next-generation system. Just three and a half years later, Microsoft unleashed the Xbox 360 into the marketplace.

Thus began the battle among these giants of industry for domination of the next generation of video gaming. It was a desperate struggle, unprecedented even in the history of videogames.

Amid that struggle, Nintendo's Wii took only one year and eight months to break the 30 million unit barrier, smashing the PS2's record of two years and two months. Nintendo was more than holding its own against its giant opponents.

By December 2008, the Wii had sold 44.96 million units worldwide—1.6 times as many as the Xbox 360, and 2.1 times the PS3. And the gap is only widening.

Of course, the battle is not over yet. Both Sony and Microsoft have countered by slashing prices, and the face of the war may still change.

For example, American market research firm IDC projects that by the end of 2012 the PS3 will narrowly edge the Wii out, reaching 110 million units, with the Wii coming in at 105 million and the Xbox 360 utterly defeated at 40 million.

But in the history of videogame consoles, control of the marketplace has usually gone to the competitor who takes the biggest market share in the shortest amount of time. The Wii's vertical ascent would seem to give it an advantage.

What's more, it has allies denied to its rivals.

The Wii is running every night in the living room of a certain home in Shizuoka prefecture. But children are not the ones playing it. An older couple—64 and 57—face the TV as they amuse themselves bowling and playing tennis with *Wii Sports*.

In the summer of 2008, to stave off aging, they bought *Wii Fit*. Using the included balance board, they follow the directions of the instructor on the screen, beginning a regimen of yoga and step-up exercises. The treadmill in the corner gets less and less attention.

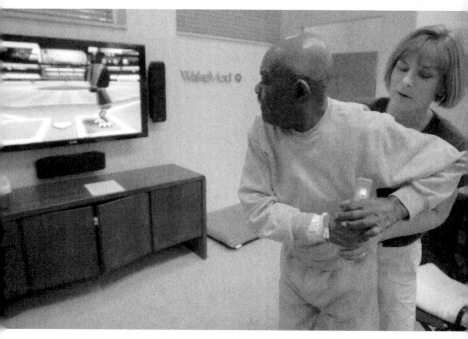

A patient engages in physical therapy using the Wii at a North Carolina medical facility. The Wii helps nurture equipoise and to train arm muscles. [Photo © Getty Images]

Elsewhere, at Wakemed Health Park—a leading physical therapy center in North Carolina, USA—a patient recovering from a cerebral hemorrhage holds a Wii controller like a baseball bat, playing games under the watchful eye of his physical therapist. Facilities like this are rapidly becoming common in the United States.

Changing locations again, the British tabloid *The People* runs a headline in January 2008: "Make way for the Q Wii N," it playfully proclaims, in a story about Queen Elizabeth's fascination with the Wii. The story goes that the Queen cut in on Prince William, who was playing a Wii he'd received as a gift from his girlfriend, and went on to monopolize the system. Evidently the Prince was quite taken with his new, "cool" grandmother.

A large portion of the Wii user base is made up of people who previously had no interest in playing videogames. The PS3 and Xbox 360 have no such advantage, but before the Wii lies a vast blue ocean of unexplored market potential.

The Wii joined in on the DS's goal of expanding the gaming population—a goal that has been favorably received by the marketplace. But for Nintendo to do this—to distance themselves from the constant pressure towards better graphics and more processing power—was a long and painful process.

The Ten Year War with Sony

Iwata recalls that Nintendo's plan to expand the gaming population came out of a long period of hard thinking amid the videogame wars.

"It wasn't like god came down one day with the revelation, 'create more gamers.' We realized something was weird about the results our efforts were getting. We argued about why people weren't playing videogames, there was a lot of trial and error, and finally we realized we were in real trouble. That was around 2002, right when I became president."

The strategy of expanding gaming's appeal—first expressed in the

Nintendo and Sony: Outcome of the Ten Year War

	On-Sale Date in Japan	Units Sold* (Japan/Global)	Software Titles** (Japan/Global)
PlayStation	Dec. 1994	21.59 million/ 124.9 million	Approx. 4,400
NINTENDO 64	Jun. 1996	5.54 million/ 32.93 million	Approx. 210
PlayStation 2	Mar. 2000	Approx. 26 million***/ Approx. 132 million	Approx. 4,550
Nintendo GameCube	Sep. 2001	4.4 million/ 21.74 million	Approx. 280

*At end of Mar 2008; **At end of Sep 2008; ***Includes Asia

DS—only came to light gradually, as the result of a bitter battle for market share in the home console domain.

The long war with Sony began with SCE's introduction of the first-generation PlayStation in 1994. The PlayStation went on to sell 100 million units worldwide. Sony, having dethroned Nintendo, solidified their victory with the PS2, emerging victorious in the Ten Year War with Nintendo.

During this period, Nintendo and Sony competed with each other to create ever-faster hardware and more spectacular graphics, dragging the evolution of game software behind them. But each company's approach was different.

The release of the PlayStation was enabled by improvements in semiconductor technology and brought videogames into the world of three dimensions. PlayStation games were distributed on CD-ROM discs, rather than cartridges; the amount of data contained jumped from a few megabytes to a few hundred megabytes. This induced videogames to become massive in many ways.

Games that incorporated live action or fully animated cut scenes became more common, and the 3-D graphics and high-quality sound fascinated a generation that had gotten used to the bleeps and bloops of the older Nintendo systems. At the same time, the large data capacity allowed for a much wider scope within a game—games could be longer, with more characters and items. Fans bored of simple games welcomed the added complexity with open arms.

Nintendo countered in June 1996, a year and a half after the introduction of the original PlayStation. The company may have taken longer to step up to the 3-D wars, but its response was a monster of a console called the Nintendo 64.

The 64 had graphical processing power comparable to the supercomputers of the day, which gave it an advantage when rendering complicated movements in three dimensions. The imagery it generated was far superior to its rival, the PlayStation.

"Games will change, the 64 will change them," went the catchphrase, and it was an appropriate one. Players could manipulate their in-game viewpoint at will, and the way the immersive graphics would shift to keep up stunned industry insiders. It seemed to promise a new era of videogames. But this performance came with a price.

When it came to using the machine's processing power—said to be four times the PlayStation's—and creating games that made use of the newly immersive abilities of the system, old ideas and methods were worthless. Development time and effort skyrocketed.

"If you can't keep up, that's not our problem," Nintendo seemed to say. Their naively single-minded pursuit of new and interesting games, of quality over quantity, resulted in a platform that presented an extremely high barrier to entry to software developers. The difficult hardware was like a challenge flung at the feet of anyone who wanted to create a game for it.

Of course, the PlayStation also faced the issues of increasing development effort and cost. But its hardware was less advanced than the 64's and aimed only to enhance the prevailing gaming experience; Sony took great pains to create an inexpensive development environment, which lowered the barrier to entry for software makers. As a result, developers who were unable to manage the 64's monstrous power flocked to the PlayStation, and the gap in the number of games available for each system grew.

At the end of 1997, a year and a half after the 64's introduction, there were only a little more than 50 titles available for the system. By contrast, there were over 1000 on the PlayStation. The home game system market was now firmly in Sony's control.

They enabled the creation of games much like those that already existed, but with the improved graphics and sound one would expect from an electronics giant. In March of 2000, they released the PlayStation 2, a successor designed to pursue the same philosophy of massive enhancement. The PS2 used DVD-ROM discs that held over six times as much data as the old CD-ROMs, and it could play DVD movies as well.

Meanwhile, the 64 sold only 5.54 million units in Japan and 32.93 million worldwide. Nintendo was faced with difficult choices in developing its successor.

Quitting Games: The Impending Crisis

In August of 2000, five months after Sony's PS2 launched to immense popularity (along with constant shortages), Nintendo at last officially introduced their competing home console, which had been under development for some time under the codename "Dolphin." The new system—dubbed the Nintendo GameCube—was small, even cute, like some petite piece of stereo equipment. It seemed designed specifically to distance itself from the 64.

"The Lessons of the 64"—that was the phrase that Genyo Takeda, then-general manager of Nintendo's integrated research division and head of hardware development, used during his presentation. It was clear that he was proud of the way Nintendo had taken the failings of the 64 fully to heart.

The 64, with its uncompromisingly powerful hardware, was difficult even for Nintendo's own software developers. When the 64 launched in June 1996, just two games had been developed for it. Only two more would be released in time for the end-of-year sales season six months later. The slow development cycle was proof of the high demands the system placed on developers.

By contrast, the GameCube was designed to make game development as easy as possible, rather than aiming for peak computational power. Put another way, it was designed to let developers pursue the appeal of gaming itself. It went on sale in September of 2001.

Abandoning the 64's cartridge format, the GameCube was the first Nintendo system to use an optical drive. The custom 8 cm DVD-based discs were manufactured in cooperation with Matsushita (now Panasonic). The new discs were cheaper, and where 64 games cost 9,800 yen, software for the GameCube was pushed down to 6,800 yen, much closer to the average price for PlayStation games.

The GameCube had indeed benefited from the lessons learned from the 64, but it had still inherited Nintendo's fixation on games, the fun of gaming itself. Software bloated with huge movie and sound files were out; the smaller 8 cm discs held less data and discouraged that avenue. The GameCube was meant to stand in contrast to the PS2, the home appliance that happened to run games but could also play the DVD movies that were just starting to become common in the marketplace at the time. At the GameCube's unveiling, Takeda spoke about the system's intense focus on games. "This is the best game system ever created," he said. "We're not trying to dominate other fields like some other companies."

But in the end the GameCube finished its life below even the 64, totally unable to compete with the PS2. It sold a total of 4.04 million units in Japan, compared with the 64's 5.54 million. Worldwide, it sold 21.74 million—Nintendo's worst-performing home console to date.

On the other hand, the PS2 sold 10 million units in Japan and 30 million worldwide within two years of its release, and by the end of 2005 that figure broke 100 million.

"Even now, I value the GameCube's design ideals and output. It was clearly easier to develop for than the 64. But that wasn't enough to solve the problem, and there was actually something else happening at the same time," says Iwata—and it's true that the GameCube was a well-made system. It allowed for efficient development, and at the end of its lifetime there were roughly 280 titles available for it in Japan—more than there ever were for the 64, despite the GameCube's lower sales. The console's high quality is evident, especially considering that much of its design would be reused for the Wii.

But there was Iwata's "something else," and it stood in the way of "the best game system ever created."

In 2000, at the beginning of the second round of the Ten Year War, the videogame software business was losing its former vigor.

Hardware was selling, but not games. According to the Computer Entertainment Supplier's Association (CESA), from January to December 2000, thanks to the release of the PS2 that year, hardware shipments totaled 189.2 billion yen, double the previous year's figure. Software, on the other hand, was down 11% to 293.1 billion yen. The release of the GameCube the following year boosted hardware shipments again, but it had no effect on declining software sales, which fell another 10%.

Many industry insiders were willing to dismiss this as a temporary lull created by a transition in hardware. But Iwata saw it differently.

"It was all too easy for us to heed the voices of enthusiastic fans who bought lots of games. But we started to wonder if the result of crafting games just for that audience was that the gaming population as a whole was shrinking."

The realization sank in just as Iwata became president of the company, in 2002. Immediately upon taking the helm from Yamauchi, his first priority was arriving at a clear, objective understanding of what was happening to the game industry—and the conclusion was that the abandoning of games had reached a serious point.

Says Iwata, "We did a lot of thinking and investigating, but no matter how we looked at it, fewer people were playing games. It wasn't that children weren't playing videogames any more—but they were graduating from them earlier. It used to be that they'd come home early and have plenty of time to play, but that time had disappeared from society as a whole. The result of all our hard work to make wonderful games was that people without the time or energy to devote

Shift in Japanese Gaming Market

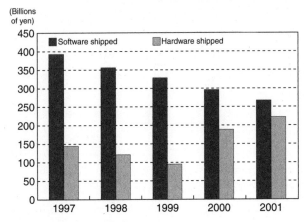

Source: 2002 CESA White Paper on Gaming

to them were just saying 'heck with it' and walking away. The more we investigated this, the more severe we realized the problem was."

Even around Iwata himself, fewer and fewer people were playing videogames. He made a point of asking visiting journalists, "So, have you played a videogame lately?" Most of them scratched their head sheepishly and confessed, "I used to play before, but these days..."

Everyone in the game industry assumed that the prettier a game's graphics were, the more challenge and length it offered, the more people would like it. But that trend in gaming wasn't satisfying everyone's needs. Iwata had come to a realization.

Why was the PS2 so successful? Iwata decided that it was selling not because of its capability as a game system, but rather on its ability to play DVDs. Its initial retail price was 39,800 yen. It was high, for a game system, but DVD players cost between half and two-thirds as much, and the PS2 could also play previously purchased PlayStation games. It wasn't like the old days, where people would buy a game system because they just *had* to play games.

The writing was clear as to what the new president had to do.

In September 2003, the Tokyo Game Show (Asia's largest game industry event) was held at at Makuhari Messe International Convention Center in Chiba prefecture. Iwata was delivering the keynote address; the theme was "20 years after the Nintendo Famicom: The Past, Present, and Future of the Videogame Industry."

As he looked back on the history of the industry, Iwata explained how and why the audience for videogames was shrinking, finally stating: "They've given up on videogames; we have to call them back in."

It was the first time the head of Nintendo both articulated the sense of crisis the company felt, and declared their intent to solve the problem—a conclusion he'd arrived at in a year of trying to decide the direction the company would take.

By this time, the company's first response—the Nintendo DS— had reached the prototype stage. Preparations for their counteroffensive had begun.

2

The Birth of the DS and the Wii

"What's important isn't next-generation technology, but next-generation game experiences. Computing power isn't that big of a deal."

—Iwata

The DS, Born in a Restaurant

One day in the spring of 2003, Iwata went out for Italian food, taking Nintendo's chief of software development, Shigeru Miyamoto, with him. There was a 116-booth, 250-yard driving range a few minutes' walk from Nintendo's headquarters in Kyoto, and on the range's second floor was a place called "Chiasso," whose lunches Iwata liked. They were delicious and reasonably priced.

At the time, the two of them were agonizing over what to do about the next-generation handheld system they were about to build.

It had been the company's Game Boy series of portable game systems that supported it during the decade of a losing war with Sony. Before he retired, the former president of Nintendo, Yamauchi, had left them with a single hint regarding the new system: "You oughtta do one with two screens."

Twin screens, though, seemed to suggest more complicated games that would appeal to advanced, experienced players. It was nothing but a source of worry for the two men. It seemed like an impossible demand until Miyamoto solved the problem with a single utterance at that lunch.

"It'd be neat if one of the screens were a touch display, wouldn't it?"

The 64 and GameCube represented a slump in the company's home console business that lasted two hardware generations, but on the portable Game Boy systems, the *Pokémon* series of videogames was massively popular. 2001 saw the introduction of the Game Boy's successor, the Game Boy Advance, which secured for Nintendo an uncontested position at the top of the portable game market.

But success in the portable domain did not bring with it any peace. People were still leaving games behind, whether they were portable or not.

In 2002, after succeeding the presidency of Nintendo and realizing the grave nature of the crisis, Iwata started by talking about it.

The one he talked to the most was Miyamoto, famed designer of games like *Zelda* and *Super Mario Bros.*, and general manager of Nintendo Entertainment Analysis and Development. They needed to develop a new hardware platform from scratch—one that would help stop the trend that threatened their business. To do that, Miyamoto's exhaustive experience with software was indispensable.

"What's keeping people from touching game machines? What's making them run away?"

Their discussions started there. Recent game systems had button-encrusted controllers that were too complicated. Software that used complicated technology was becoming more common, and the gap between experienced players and beginners was growing wider all the time. It scared people off—or worse, made them actively dislike videogames. Their discussions grew to encompass the themes of games.

While adventure games like *Mario* were fine, was that really enough? What if games included themes that related to the lives of ordinary people? Would people who considered gaming a waste of time embrace it then? As they converged on the company's new direction, the idea came to Miyamoto: dedicate one of the displays to touch control.

One screen would be used for intuitive, approachable controls, and the other would be the main display. The system would be easy for anyone to control, and it would allow the development of new kinds of games.

Miyamoto immediately set to work to come up with prototype hardware that would resemble, in outward form, the "Game & Watch" series of electronic games that had set Nintendo down its electronics path in the early 1980s, yet represent a radically different concept.

In the summer of 2003 Miyamoto showed Iwata a new PDA. It was called a PocketPC and had started to gain popularity among businessmen with its stylus-based input system.

The small device allowed users to manage their contacts, email, and calendar using either an on-screen keyboard or handwriting recognition. Miyamoto had stuck a strip of tape across the middle of the screen, dividing it into two halves—a kind of makeshift dual screen.

Yet there on the screen was Mario. He dropped down from the top of the display; touching him with the pen made him jump into the air. It was an uncomplicated piece of software.

"Hey, this is great!"

"Isn't it?"

Iwata and Miyamoto beamed at the simple controls for the simple game. It was the moment that crystallized the basic design for the Nintendo DS.

It was only a few months earlier that Sony Computer Entertainment—the company that dominated the home console marketplace—had announced that they were getting into portable game systems as well.

"We'd like to welcome the newest member of the PlayStation family: The PSP. It's a portable PlayStation."

Held annually in the United States, E3—the Electronic Entertainment Expo—is the largest videogame industry event in the world. In May 2003, SCE president Ken Kutaragi had spoken those words, and taken a tiny optical disc called a UMD, or Universal Media Disc, from his pocket. The PSP would be the first portable game system to use an optical drive. It would carry two powerful CPUs, with processing power roughly equivalent to the PS2.

Kutaragi promised to "show the system itself at next year's E3, and have it on sale worldwide by the end of next year." Nintendo's stock took a major blow at the introduction of this so-called "21st Century Walkman" that could not only play games but also music and movies. Investors couldn't help but have visions of the past when Sony stole huge chunks of Nintendo's home console business. The pressure was on.

But Iwata was unmoved; while Sony chased processing power, Nintendo would head in another direction entirely.

In August 2003, once the basic design for the DS was decided, Iwata launched a small counterattack at a corporate strategy briefing attended by journalists and analysts. "I can't reveal any details," he said, "but Nintendo is heading for growth in a new direction. We're working on something completely new that anyone might pick up."

Early the next year, in January 2004, Nintendo revealed that they would be launching a twin-screened portable system at the end of that year—the same time as the PSP. In May they demonstrated the hardware before an excited audience at E3. It was the first time the public saw the fruits of Nintendo's efforts to increase the gaming population, and the media reported on the new system with breathless anticipation.

"This direction is the right one." Iwata's increasing confidence was being reflected in the development of another strategic product.

Mom Has To Like It: The Development of the Wii

In the first half of 2003, when Iwata and Miyamoto were dreaming up designs for the Nintendo's new dual-screened portable system, they were also deep in discussions with the head of integrated research, Takeda, about a new home game system.

Takeda was Nintendo's hardware pro, responsible for the development of every home game system from the NES to the GameCube—but this time, Iwata had given him new orders.

"Takeda, listen—this time we can't just focus on making a more powerful system."

"So you're telling me to go off the tech roadmap?" Takeda asked.

"That's right. Let's get off it."

It went against every piece of received wisdom in the videogame industry.

Computers optimized for playing videogames—and especially home videogame systems—have significant overlap with advancements in general-purpose computing. From the chips that served as their CPUs and graphics processors, to optical media like DVDs, to wireless networking—the list goes on and on. The desperate competition for supremacy in the home console domain led manufacturers to the bleeding edge of technological advancement.

It was common sense, then, that console makers would plan their hardware development along the expected path of technological advancement—the "technology roadmap."

Nintendo was no exception. They had embodied the state of the art with the 64, and even though its successor, the GameCube, had not been designed solely for raw performance, it was far more powerful than the 64. The GameCube had straightforwardly incorporated advancements in technology made since the 64. The Wii's debut was fully five years after the GameCube's. It was only reasonable that it would include five years' worth of technological advancements.

But now Iwata was telling Takeda to stop planning designs based solely on technological progress. What he was suggesting now was an entirely new approach; it was something that had never been tried before.

Instead of designing a console around fundamental performance, the new system would expressly seek out technology that would endear itself to families—a "Mom has to like it" approach to development.

"Videogames drive Mom crazy—she has to pick up the controllers once the kids are done playing, they've already got multiple consoles plugged into the TV and she doesn't want another one. They're a nuisance, as far as she's concerned. We realized that if we wanted to grow the gaming population, we had to build a console that no one in the family hated."

Mom didn't care about processing speed, so using technology as the starting point was meaningless. So what *did* Mom care about? They would determine the Wii's specifications to appeal to a mom's sensibility.

Compared with its rivals, the PS3 and Xbox 360, the Wii is significantly smaller. Viewed end-on, the area of the main unit's front panel is less than half of either the PS3's or Xbox's, and it takes up only one-sixth the volume of the PS3, and one-fifth that of the Xbox.

This was the first thing Iwata had fixated on.

It started during a meeting Iwata had with Miyamoto and Takeda.

They'd gotten as far as "don't chase performance" and "Mom has to like it" when Iwata said "Hang on just a second," and suddenly left his office. He returned with several common DVD clamshell cases. He stacked two, then three of them together.

"Our next-generation machine shouldn't be any bigger than two or three DVD boxes."

Every manufacturer's consoles had gotten bigger with each generation, as if to display their increased capabilities. Yet Iwata was now saying their next home console would be smaller even than the original NES.

From the standpoint of appealing to Mom, though, Iwata thought it made good sense.

A smaller console would feel less like extra clutter. In order to avoid overheating, the compact design would require the hardware to use less electricity, which would make it more economical to run. If they could control the heat problem, that meant the console wouldn't need a noisy cooling fan.

Raw computing power was completely antithetical to the triple virtues of compact size, low power consumption, and quiet operation. Nintendo had sworn to increase the gaming population, and it was clear which direction they would choose.

However, hardware engineers who dislike high performance are rare. It would be quite difficult not to care what their rivals were up to. Sony was in the midst of developing their next-generation system, the PS3, whose main selling point would be its supercomputer-like processing speed. Its custom-made Cell Processor utilized the latest in semiconductor miniaturization technology to fit nine CPUs on a single chip.

Microsoft, too, was working with IBM to increase the capabilities of the PowerPC chips that would power its Xbox 360 system, which would be many times as powerful as its predecessor. The first manufacturer to use the PowerPC CPU in a game console had been none other than Nintendo.

Their rivals were pressing onward. Iwata was convinced that there was no future in pursuing pure computing power, but the group of engineers that Takeda led were bound to be worried.

When Takeda was asked about doubts and concerns he may have had, he answered, "I can't say we didn't have any. We're engineers, after all. We'd think about things like wouldn't there still be a certain market for a faster machine, or whether it was okay to be taking a gamble like this. When an order comes down to do something different, not having a specific solution, no counterproposal, makes everyone anxious of course."

But early in the development stages, Takeda realized that "this was just directing our engineering efforts in another direction. It wasn't as though we were abandoning engineering altogether."

It was like designing a laptop computer. To fit the necessary components into such a small enclosure, designs became more complicated and more expensive. To hit the three goals of small size, low power consumption, and quiet operation without sacrificing *too* much processing capability and keeping costs down would take serious engineering acumen.

"It might seem like game console design is a unique field, but if you look at larger trends it has a lot in common with computer or cell phone engineering. You're on a prescribed playing field. What's the point of doing the same thing as everybody else?"

Takeda put the challenge to his team of engineers, and they set about designing the CPU, which would be the most power-hungry component in the system.

In order to control costs and avoid chasing technology for its own sake, the next-generation system would be based on an updated, improved version of the GameCube hardware. So long as the basic structure remained the same, it would be compatible with GameCube software. After all, one of the main selling points of the PS2 was that it could play games written for the original PlayStation.

The first goal for the engineering team was to find out by how much they could lower power consumption while preserving GameCube-like levels of performance.

Semiconductors allow circuit pathways to be made narrower so that more of them can be fit on a given chip, thereby increasing processing power. With more circuits in the same area, the amount of current flowing through the chip rises, producing more heat—but Nintendo used this law against itself.

Instead of fitting more, narrower circuit pathways on a chip, they scaled the same chip down to shrink power consumption and heat.

At the time, 180 nanometer (that is to say, 180 billionths of a meter) pathways were standard; the GameCube was no exception. But the major semiconductor manufacturers like Intel and IBM were already developing 90 nanometer chips, which would be ready for volume production right about the time the next generation of game consoles would be going on sale.

What if Nintendo's new system used a 90-nanometer version of the GameCube CPU? Based on their research, the development team found that one third to one fourth the power use of the old chip was a feasible goal. While their rivals were using the new technology to ask "How much can we boost performance?" Nintendo was asking "How much can we shrink power consumption?"

The efforts to lower power use didn't stop with the CPU—they extended into every aspect of the unit, from the graphics processor to the wireless networking, to overall physical structure. As a result, the team's confidence that they would be able to fulfill Iwata's reckless goal of a system "no bigger than two or three DVD boxes" was deepening.

As he watched the ongoing efforts, Iwata's confidence, too, grew—confidence that they would be able to deliver, in the wake of the DS, a new kind of home console too.

In June 2004—only a month after the DS debuted at E3 and shocked the world with its novel concepts—Iwata announced at a corporate strategy briefing in Japan that Nintendo was in the process of developing a new home console.

"What's important isn't next-generation technology, but next-generation game experiences. Computing power isn't that big of a deal. At this year's E3, we introduced the DS, with a design unlike anything that's come before it. With our next home console, we'll be doing the same thing, and you'll see it at next year's E3. Inside the company, it's been code-named 'Revolution.'"

Iwata had already shown Nintendo's first concrete step toward bringing people back to gaming—and now he was calling the next step a "revolution." The name was meant to evoke the surprise that people felt the first time they played the original NES, with intuitive gameplay à la DS that anyone could engage.

The idea to bring innovative gameplay to users already existed, but it would be another six months before that concept was turned to reality.

The Humble Remote Control

For the Revolution to live up to its codename and revolutionize the game industry by expanding the gaming population, it would need something special.

The DS, with its dual screens and stylus controls, lowered the barrier to videogames. The Revolution needed to do the same thing. The controller would be at the core of its interface, and it could not be less than perfect.

Certain aspects of the controller were decided early in its development: It had to be wireless, and it could not be intimidating.

When Iwata was talking to Miyamoto and company about the circumstances that were leading to gaming's decline, the first thing that came to the president's mind was a TV remote control—a piece of technology the entire family used.

People who didn't play videogames never touched game controllers. The wires that snaked out from the console were nothing but a nuisance to them, and if controllers dared to be left about, they were put away. But the TV remote never bothered anybody. As Iwata considered the difference between the two, he realized the new controller would have to be wireless.

Then he wondered if people found controllers intimidating because of the way they looked.

Game controllers were constantly getting more complicated; in addition to the standard direction pad and buttons, they were now encrusted with all manner of analog control sticks and triggers, placed seemingly everywhere. Was that alone enough, perhaps, to drive people away from a videogame?

The new controller had to be simple and approachable. Iwata also felt that, like the DS's touch screen, it needed to facilitate direct, intuitive controls—and Miyamoto and Takeda agreed.

It was an easy goal to set, but a hard one to reach.

Development on the new controller was in full swing by the middle of 2004. With Iwata focusing on the DS, Miyamoto acted in his place on the project. Takeda's engineering team searched for sensors that would enable intuitive game control, which Miyamoto's people used to implement the actual controller.

At first, they started just as Iwata had suggested—by aiming for a simple, TV remote-like controller. But as they did the work of testing the controller prototypes that included the new sensors, the form factors began to take unexpected directions.

"No one liked that one," recalls Miyamoto with a rueful grin, of a large, disc-shaped example. It had a large star-shaped button in the center, surrounded by three smaller buttons, and used internal accelerometers that let the player control by tilting it forward, backwards, left, or right. The prototype was orange, and its bizarre appearance earned it the nickname "cheddar cheese" from the development team.

It was admittedly simple and easy to understand, but it was also far too garish. Miyamoto's team met with around 40 game developers within Nintendo bimonthly to hear their opinions. This iteration of the controller met with opposition—they complained that it was totally unsuited to traditional games like *Mario* and *Zelda*.

Meanwhile, the search continued for something equivalent to the DS that might involve the idea of touching.

The development team was fixated on a pointing device that would allow direct, obvious interaction with the screen—something like a computer's mouse. "We might still use it in the future so I can't say much," said Miyamoto, but it seems that touch pads not unlike the type used on many laptop computers were seriously considered.

The team went through dozens of prototypes—some were truly fantastic, with pointing devices on the front and traditional two-handed button controls on the back. But it wasn't direct enough—touching the controller *here* affected the screen *there*. It wasn't intuitive.

But then Takeda arrived with a sensor that saved the day.

"Here, give this a try. It's really responsive."

It was near the end of 2004, roughly six months since controller development had begun in earnest, when Takeda demonstrated a new prototype.

It used camera components—specifically, a CMOS imaging sensor of the kind widely used in video cameras. By using the sensor to track the position of two light sources placed near the TV, the controller could calculate the direction in which it was pointing.

A normal video camera captures between 30 and 60 images per second. That was fast enough to fool the human eye, but for the controller to keep up with fast-moving gameplay, standard imaging speeds wouldn't be fast enough. But since the system Takeda had devised had only to track two discrete points of light, it was able to sample images at over 200 frames per second and send the resulting positional information to the console. A dark horse had appeared in the race to complete the controller.

"It's a cinch tracking the motion." "Since you're pointing it at the TV, it matches up with where you're looking—it just feels right." "If we make this the core of the unit along with standard controls, you'll be able to enjoy traditional games, too."

Praise rolled in from the development team—and it solved the form factor problem as well.

Since the controller had to be pointed at the TV, it was natural to hold it vertically, like a TV remote. Fitting it with accelerometers allowed it to sense movements like tilting and shaking as well. Careful arrangement of the buttons on the unit meant that it could be held sideways and used as a more traditional game controller. In addition to solving all these problems, the new design had settled into something very close to Iwata's original ideal of a TV remote.

For the controller development team, it felt like the fog that covered the path ahead had finally lifted.

Thus was the Wii born—with an intuitive controller that you could shake and direct at a desired point on the screen.

It would make the system approachable for anyone, even parents and grandparents who never played videogames. By Iwata's insistence, it became the first videogame controller to be dubbed a "remote."

The Wii development team's next challenge would be to turn the system that nobody in the family would hate into the system that everybody in the family would love.

Something New Every Day

The Wii's public unveiling at E3 in May 2005 was just a few weeks away. Iwata was in his office, agonizing over the content of the presentation. To show off the "new kind of home console" he had promised at the previous year's corporate strategy briefing, he would have to offer specifics on the Revolution's design. The hardware specification had solidified, and the controller was mostly complete. In order to have something to demo at E3, Miyamoto and his team were now hard at work writing a variety of sample games like fishing and tennis—and in actual play, the games felt right.

The DS was selling well in Japan, outpacing SCE's PSP, which had gone on sale at roughly the same time. The puppy-raising game *Nintendogs* was popular. Nintendo's efforts to grow the gaming population seemed to be well-received by the marketplace, and Iwata felt that they would be able to present the Wii with confidence.

But then Iwata decided to stop short of unveiling the new concepts embodied in the controller, instead giving only an outline of the console itself, along with its only-just-finalized enclosure design.

It was bitter experience that led to this decision—Nintendo's

ideas had been copied before. When they had demonstrated the 64
controller's vibration capability, Sony had beaten them to the market
with it.

And there was another reason—there was something they had
to do before Iwata felt fully confident about unveiling the Wii to the
public.

"Unobtrusive." "Unintimidating." "Impossible to hate."

The first phase of the Wii's hardware development, which concerned
the specs, focused on removing all of the negative implications that
came with a game console. Just as in the DS, they were able to break
with tradition and create a new interface that everyone could approach
with equal ease.

But that wasn't enough to satisfy Iwata.

"The more positive feedback we got on the DS, the more we asked
questions like 'do we need a home console at all?' Some of the stuff
would have terrified Takeda had he heard them. [laugh] It's no good
if the only difference is the home console using a big LCD screen, and
the portable using a small one. We had many discussions about the
specific appeal and *raison d'être* of a home console," he said.

Once the basic design for the controller had been settled in early
2005, Iwata gave the following memo to Miyamoto and Takeda: "I
want the Wii to be a machine that gives you more channels on your
TV."

Compared with a portable game system that could be easily
flipped on and used to kill a few minutes, a home console required
stronger motive to start up and use. Naturally they would develop
games like *Nintendogs* and *Brain Age* that anyone could enjoy, but that
alone would not be enough.

The TV was common property in a typical household. There were
programs that everyone watched together, and programs just for kids.
If shows happened to overlap, there could even be quarrels over who
would get to watch what they wanted. The goal for the Wii was the
same—for it to have something for everyone in the family, for it to be
a channel that someone would want to watch every day. That was the

true *raison d'être* of a home console, and that was what Iwata meant with his memo.

And again it was Takeda who rose to the challenge.

What Takeda suggested was the idea of "something new every day." Every time the system was powered up, it needed to display something new, something that would interest the whole family—like a weather report or news story.

Internet connectivity had always been a basic criterion for the Wii's design, and if it were constantly updating itself, it could be a new machine every time it was turned on.

A variety of such projects existed within Nintendo—projects that were dependent on specific features of the unit. Previously, the hardware would be designed and completed, then work could begin on the software that used said hardware. But now the hardware would need to come with a variety of software components already installed. The development of the Wii involved both hardware and software, and the two were inextricably linked.

In October 2005, Iwata formed a group that he called "the most interconnected in the history of Nintendo." He gathered 25 top talents from departments throughout the company for a group called the "Console Functions Team."

The team's job started with the design of the screen that would be displayed as soon as the Wii was powered up.

A user might want to do any number of things—play a game from a disc they'd inserted, play a downloaded game, check the weather, read news headlines. A good number of console functions were already available, but the problem was displaying the options in a simple, understandable fashion.

Then one of the team members thought of a row of TVs all lined up, like you might see in any electronics store. From that vision was born the design of the startup menu, which looks like a grid of small TV screens of the same size.

Prior to that, it was common sense that if a game disc was inserted into the unit and it was turned on, the game would launch automatically. The Console Functions Team not only had the Wii display a menu screen, but also didn't even make the game item any bigger than any other option. Games were treated the same as every other feature, so that non-gamers would be able to see the options available for them.

Another team member took one look at the screen and said, "It looks like channels on TV."

The main menu was thus naturally given the name "Wii Channel." Said Iwata: "All I did was mention 'channels' as one of the concepts of the Wii. The Console Functions Team went and came up with that name. It seems like a total coincidence, but in the end we were all aiming for the same goal."

The Console Functions Team was concerned with how the Wii would fit into family life, and features designed to facilitate that sprang up one after another. The most conspicuous was the Wii Message Board, a bulletin board-like feature that allowed family members to leave messages for each other. The inspiration was the surface of a refrigerator, where Mom would leave notes for the kids. Messages on the board looked like notes stuck to a real bulletin board, complete with pin.

The Message Board also recorded gameplay history, showing the play times and scores of games played on the console. Play history could not be deleted—Iwata had been adamant about this.

He felt so strongly about games being a healthy part of the lives of the whole family that he suggested, "How about the system shutting itself off after an hour if the parents decide that their children can only play an hour a day?" It was an unthinkable proposal, coming from the mouth of the president of a videogame company.

Aside from the message board, the Console Functions Team developed a host of other channels designed to bring the family together.

There was the Photo Channel, which would display slideshows of photographs taken with any digital camera, complete with background music—and the Mii Channel, where users could create caricatures of themselves and their family and friends, which could then appear as characters in games.

Channels like News and Weather, that needed to receive new information daily, were developed in conjunction with a feature called WiiConnect24, which allowed the console to connect to the internet even while powered down in standby mode.

To enable this feature, Takeda and his engineers were faced with the daunting task of building a truly low power consumption machine that never slept.

Low power consumption and low-heat operation were basic design requirements in order to meet the goal of being no bigger than two or three DVD cases. Staying powered on 24 hours a day represented an even higher hurdle.

A basic tenet of the Wii's design was mom-friendliness. The concept of WiiConnect24 was good, but if it made Mom angry, it was back to square one. If the unit were to run all night, it had to use very little power, and operation noise would also be an issue. Iwata kept on saying, "You can't have the fan run while it's in standby at night. If Mom hears that fan, she'll pull the plug." To people who understood the engineering involved, it was an absurd requirement, one that bordered on the impossible. But Takeda and crew pulled it off.

The component that contributed the most to the system's low power consumption was the tiny CPU, which had a surface area of only 18.9 square millimeters. Despite the fact that it delivered roughly twice the processing power of the GameCube's CPU, it was half the size, which kept both heat and power consumption down. For comparison, the PS3's CPU's surface area measures 228 square millimeters—over ten times larger. When playing games, it uses over ten times as much power.

Thanks to the efficient CPU, and the myriad other small improvements to the system, Takeda's engineering team succeeded in preserving the ability to transfer data over the network while in standby mode, using—in his words—"no more power than a miniature bulb."

According to one study, the Wii's power consumption while using WiiConnect24 is a mere nine watts per hour, or equivalent to running nine small Christmas tree lights. When calculated against the average cost of electricity in Japan (22 yen per kilowatt/hour) it costs a mere 1,730 yen to power the Wii over the course of a year. Playing it five hours a day only brings that figure to 2,000 yen. The PS3 and Xbox 360 cost 8,000 yen a year to run—quadruple what the Wii costs. The difference in power consumption is staggering.

This only makes Nintendo's goal for the Wii that much clearer. It was designed to relate to the whole family—to show them something new every day.

In May 2006, at E3, Nintendo revealed to the world their Revolution—now the Wii.

At Kodak Theatre—the venue for the Academy Awards—Miyamoto was the first on stage, holding a Wii Remote. The audience looked on, holding its collective breath.

Finally Iwata came on stage, and explained everything in his own words, from the Wii Remote to WiiConnect24. He finished with this bold statement:

"Something new every day. Something for everyone, every day. This is our answer."

The theatre exploded in applause for two geniuses—Iwata and Miyamoto.

3

Iwata and Miyamoto: Business Ascetics

"On my business card, I'm a company president... But my mind's that of a game developer... And at heart, I am a gamer."

—Iwata

"Sending text messages is way more fun for them than any game we make. If we made a game where you have to type a certain message as fast as possible and competed nationwide, that'd probably be the most fun game in Japan."

—Miyamoto

Don't Sit on Your Laurels

On June 27, 2008, at 10 AM, over 500 shareholders were assembled at Nintendo corporate headquarters in Kyoto, Japan. They had come to the white, fortress-like building to participate in the shareholders' meeting for the 2007 fiscal year.

The assembled shareholders first heard a short audit report from the auditor, then Iwata began his business presentation. Sales, operating profit, net profit—all were at record highs. The Wii had contributed significantly. Their DS business was running on all cylinders, and the number of game titles that had sold a million copies or more had doubled from the previous year and were now up to 57.

There was nothing to complain about. Yet Iwata stood there solemnly, and during the question-and-answer session, he said, "There's an inherent risk of complacency setting in. As a result of our customers' support we've been blessed with a tailwind, but people in the company are going to start taking it for granted. I'm trying to figure out how to nip that in the bud."

No matter how long their success might continue, Iwata wanted to keep the company both hungry and humble.

When he assumed the presidency of Nintendo, his strategy was to try to increase the gaming population. The plan brought Nintendo explosive profits over a very short period of time. This success was derived from basic economic principles, and it's easy to see Iwata as a brilliant strategist, in this light.

Nintendo's traditional marketplace was a proverbial sea of blood—Iwata realized there was no future in fighting a war for the territory Microsoft and Sony were determined to claim, and instead set a course for less troubled waters—that is to say, people who don't play videogames. Therein lay their success, or so the analysis goes.

But Iwata says this: "It would be cool if I could say 'Yeah, I knew it all along!' about what's happening now, but that's just not true. Even though I had confidence that our direction was the right one, the truth is I had no idea things were going to happen the way they did, as quickly as they did. On the contrary, it made me think, wow, when things change, they sure change fast. I still can't be sure what it is that will make people react strongly to what we do."

Iwata can say this with a straight face because rather than working for results, he'd done what he thought was right; the results had followed.

The right thing to do was to stop players from deserting games, and to bring videogames to a wider audience. To do that, they had to honestly engage the question: How do we make a console that won't be considered a nuisance, and how do we make a console that has something to offer everyone in the family?

Even though the path they'd chosen had won the approval of the marketplace and exceeded all expectations, they could not afford to become self-satisfied or change their strategy. To put it another way, they couldn't get cocky.

For example, the Wii represented the first piece of fully internet-capable business infrastructure Nintendo had sold, and it opened up two possible revenue streams. One was the Wii Channel.

The Wii Channel—with its ability to display up to 48 different services, from news and weather reports to television schedules—was more internet portal than game console.

By the end of 2008, Wii sales in Japan totaled some 7.8 million units. About 40% of those were connected to the internet. With 3.1 million units online, we could call the Wii the biggest TV portal in Japan. Looking abroad, that number rose to 18 million units. It was surely the single most successful TV-based portal service in the world.

As people flocked to it, the value of the platform rose. It was natural that other companies would become interested in providing content for the Wii Channel, even if it meant sharing revenue with Nintendo. Fujifilm was one such company—the first to maintain an independent channel on the Wii.

The Digicam Print Channel, added in July 2008, allows users to upload photos stored on an SD card and order prints directly from Fujifilm. It wasn't just prints—the service included a variety of Nintendo-like touches, allowing users to purchase whole albums of their photos decorated with images from games like the *Super Mario* series, or order business cards with their Mii avatars.

There were other companies that want to use this new infrastructure for online transactions.

"Moms would like it if they could get information on the sales at the local supermarket." "It'd be great for the family if they could order in-season produce from other regions."

Retail giant Seven & I Holdings, online shopping mall Rakuten, and others—they have all taken interest in the Wii Channel, and the possibilities seem endless. In addition to the usage fees Nintendo can collect, hidden within the Wii is the potential for staggering advertising revenue.

However, when confronted with such possibilities, Iwata's reaction was not what you'd expect.

"I think that calling the Wii Channel a new revenue stream smacks of counting the chickens before they've hatched, and anyway—that's not why we created it. It might turn out to be something besides a game that brings in money for the company, but that's all."

In the end, the Wii Channel was created to answer the questions "How can the Wii offer something to everyone in the family?" and "How can we get someone to turn it on every day?" Iwata says that using it as a source of revenue is purely secondary.

"We think there's a tendency in internet businesses to give daydreams and visions too much priority. People should wait until their site actually starts getting 30 million viewers worldwide every day before thinking about how to monetize."

What opportunities for revenue on the Wii channel might Nintendo itself develop for its main business? Iwata's position remained steady on the issue even regarding the Virtual Console, a game download service for the Wii.

The Virtual Console allows users to download games originally published for older consoles like the NES and 64. The games are cheap—between 500 and 1,000 yen. In late 2007, roughly a year after the launch of the Wii, the Virtual Console had sold roughly 7.8 million games, bringing in revenue of 3.5 billion yen. It doubled that figure in just three more months, as game assets that had been long unused again saw the light of day.

Yet even the Virtual Console was developed not for "revenues," but as part of Nintendo's efforts to answer the question: "Why do videogame systems get treated as unwanted guests?"

Up until the Wii, none of Nintendo's home consoles had been backwards compatible; if you wanted to play an old game, you had to keep the old console, and Mom couldn't stand seeing all those videogame systems lined up by the TV. But what if getting a Wii meant all those old machines could be put away? Thus was the Virtual Console born.

Near the beginning of the Wii's development, Iwata said to Takeda—and it wasn't clear if he was joking or not—"What if we made a console with like six slots, so you could play games from all kinds of systems?"

Takeda later agonized over this in private. Did the president mean it?

The truth was somewhere in between: "The thought was serious, but I was half-joking about the method," Iwata says. Eventually they settled on a virtual solution where games from a variety of older systems could be downloaded via the internet.

It was not unlike the "Famicon Mini," which reissued old NES games on a Game & Watch-style retro toy. They went on sale in 2004, winning success by including games that hearkened back to the NES era, appealing to both the nostalgia of adults who'd played the games as children and the frustration of those who hadn't been allowed to.

Perhaps nostalgia could be another aspect of the new game system. That possibility was the basis for the development of the Virtual Console. "We don't want to just give the games away," says Iwata flatly, "but it also isn't meant to pull in huge revenues."

At the same time, he's confident he'll get good results. "There's always the possibility that it could become an unexpectedly large revenue stream. It involves so much less energy than making a new game. I have confidence that they'll be more steadily profitable than the cell phone games a lot of game developers are working on now."

What kind of man is Satoru Iwata—that he can perfectly balance humility against unwavering confidence? A closer look is in order.

Satoru Iwata: The Heart of a Gamer

The Wii—which at the time was still known only by its codename, "Revolution"—was revealed at E3 2005, though the design of its controller would remain a secret.

Two months before that, Iwata was at the Game Developers Conference (GDC) in San Francisco. On the fourth day of the event, he took the stage after Microsoft's vice president and delivered his keynote address. He began by holding his business card up in the air.

"On my business card, I'm a company president," he began. Then he pointed to his head. "But my mind's that of a game developer." Finally, he put his hand to his chest. "And at heart, I am a gamer."

This self-introduction perfectly captured the essence of the man named Satoru Iwata, and it won the hearts of the audience in an instant.

No matter how far back we look in order to understand Iwata—who dedicated himself to broadening the gaming population, succeeded, and yet remained humble—we will find games.

He was born in Sapporo, on the northern island of Hokkaido, in December 1959. The eldest son of a prefectural official, he was brought up comfortably. He displayed leadership potential early, serving variously as class president, student council president, and club president while in middle and high school. It was while attending Sapporo South High School that he first encountered computers.

Footsteps: Satoru Iwata

TIME	EVENT
Dec. 6, 1959 (age 0)	Born in Sapporo, Hokkaido prefecture.
April 1975 (age 15)	Enters Hokkaido Sapporo South High School. As junior, learns programming for the first time.
April 1978 (age 18)	Enters Tokyo Institute of Technology in computer science. As sophomore, starts working part-time at "HAL Laboratory."
April 1982 (age 22)	Joins HAL Laboratory upon graduating college. Leads game software development.
1984 (age 24)	Makes board of directors. Begins developing software for the NES.
March 1993 (age 33)	Promoted to president. Tasked to put firm back on track with Nintendo's aid.
May 1999 (age 39)	Upon full repayment of debts, resigns to become advisor.
June 2000 (age 40)	Joins Nintendo at behest of President Hiroshi Yamauchi. Appointed to board and as head of corporate planning.
May 2002 (age 42)	Appointed president by Yamauchi.

It was regarded as the best school in the city, having turned out many graduates who went on to become well-known political and business figures. The school philosophy emphasized initiative and autonomy—it lacked even a uniform, making it a rarity among Japanese high schools. Iwata had a part-time job washing dishes, and with the money he saved up (along with some extra from his father) he bought a Hewlett-Packard HP-65 calculator.

It was the world's first programmable calculator. Introduced in 1974, it was considered a marvel of engineering, having even gone into space as a backup for the Apollo Guidance Computer during the Apollo-Soyuz Test Project.

The word "PC" hadn't even been invented yet, but already Iwata was drawn into learning how to program the tiny computer, devising games like "Volleyball" and "Missile Attack" and playing them with his classmates.

In love with computers, Iwata entered the Tokyo Institute of Technology in 1978 to study computer science. This time he used the money he received as a graduation present to buy a Commodore PET—with integrated monochrome display, keyboard, and cassette tape reader, it was the world's first all-in-one computer. He would store his programs on cassettes, and bring them every week to the Seibu department store's computer department to show off. By the time he was a sophomore, a group of the store's employees had formed a company called HAL Laboratory—and they invited Iwata to join them. It was the beginning of his career as a game designer.

The computer that appeared in Stanley Kubrick's film *2001*, "HAL," turns into "IBM" if you substitute each letter with the one that follows it in the alphabet. HAL Laboratory took their name as an homage to this—it indicated their resolve to "stay one step ahead of IBM."

It was a lofty name, but when the company was founded it had only a handful of employees who worked out of a one-room apartment in the Akihabara district of Tokyo. Its main business at the time was the development and sales of peripherals for the PCs (then called "microcomputers") that were becoming popular at the time. They had only one game programmer—Iwata, the part-timer.

Just as he was starting the job, his father, Hiroshi Iwata, won the mayoral election for the city of Muroran. In the four terms he served thereafter, he left behind him a legacy of achievement on behalf of the city, including fighting for fiscal reform, pushing through construction of the Hakucho or Swan Bridge (which straddles the Port of Muroran and is the largest suspension bridge in eastern Japan), and preserving a Nippon Steel Corporation blast furnace that was scheduled for closure.

Iwata was now the son of a mayor. He was attending a top school. But he had no interest in becoming one of the elite. He was so fascinated by games that upon graduation, he went straight to work for the unknown HAL. As the company's first videogame developer, he had no one there to learn from but continued to polish his skills on microcomputer games on his own.

The shock came in the second year of the company's operation, 1983. Nintendo unveiled their game-oriented computer, the NES (or "Famicom" as it was known in Japan). It sold for the devastatingly low price of 15,000 yen.

"Please let me write games for it."

Iwata's feet naturally took him to the company's headquarters in Kyoto. It was the beginning of a beautiful relationship.

At the time, game programmers like Iwata were still quite rare. For Nintendo, whose internal software development system was not yet sorted out, his sudden appearance was a godsend.

Golf, Pinball, F1 Race... HAL Laboratory successfully undertook software development for Nintendo to publish legendary games that supported the NES in its early days—and by doing so, the smaller company earned the larger one's trust. In 1984, Nintendo invested in HAL, underscoring HAL's importance as a crucial second-party developer.

HAL grew steadily, one employee at a time, gradually expanding the scale of its business. In addition to developing several titles for Nintendo to release under their own name, their peripherals for the NES—including controllers with autofire capability—were a hit, and they quickly became a known name in gaming. As Iwata took on more managerial responsibilities, his title changed—to board member.

But in 1992, despite its rapid growth, HAL Laboratory was faced with a crisis. They filed for bankruptcy protection under the Civil Rehabilitation Act, and were functionally insolvent.

The previous year, having grown to employ nearly 90 people, the company had moved from Tokyo to Yamanashi in an attempt to strengthen the software development section. However, it was just then that the economic bubble burst. They had borrowed most of the money to fund the new location's construction, and compounded with a recent lack of hits and the difficulty of raising short-term funding, declaring bankruptcy was the only option.

It was Nintendo that came to the rescue and supported continuing development.

Yamauchi, then president of Nintendo, had a high regard for HAL's development skills and attached a condition to Nintendo's aid: Iwata would become president of HAL upon the company's restructuring.

It was Iwata's first stint as the manager of a business—so far he'd been immersed in game creation. Though the company's outstanding liabilities had been lessened, they still owed 1.5 billion yen. Part of that debt would become Iwata's personal responsibility if the company were unable to repay it. But because his thirst to make great games had not been quenched, he trod that thorny path.

In Iwata's own words:

"I feel there's a depth, a wonder to the act of making games. Creating a single game involves constant trial and error, integrating control and play while remaining true to your theme, your concept. You wade through the vast possibilities, converging on a product. I really don't think there's anything else quite like it."

To Iwata, game design was a quest for truth. That truth could be found at the end of a long, hard development process akin to spiritual training. The endless depth of that progression captivated Iwata. Ever since high school, he had loved games more than anyone else he knew, and his desire to create them had led him here.

So despite the path of thorns—despite the great risk—Iwata had no choice but to try to turn HAL around. Once he became president, Iwata's almost simple-minded passion for creating games led to two hits for the company: 1992's *Kirby's Dream Land*, a Game Boy game, and 1999's *Super Smash Bros.* for the 64. Both were released as Nintendo games, but HAL Laboratory had developed them behind the scenes, with Iwata occasionally writing code himself to finish them.

Kirby's Dream Land was an action game featuring Kirby, a pink balloon-like creature. He could inhale enemies and items like a vacuum cleaner, then spit them back out as an attack. The new style of gameplay helped it sell five million copies, HAL's biggest hit at the time.

Nintendo and HAL would go on to produce a whopping eight more titles over the next six years, including *Kirby's Adventure* for the NES, which popularized the hero into one that stood shoulder-to-shoulder with the likes of *Mario* and *Pokémon*. The series has sold over 20 million copies worldwide.

Super Smash Bros. sold 2 million copies, the second best outing for the 64. It's a fighting game, a genre which generally involves two characters attacking each other with punches, kicks, and weapons to bring the opponent's health to zero.

But in *Smash Bros.*, the object was simply to knock your opponent out of the battle area—and battles weren't necessarily one-on-one. There might be several characters in the ring at a time—characters from other games, like Mario, Donkey Kong, and Kirby. A new genre had been born.

By making hits out of these eccentric titles, HAL had paid back its 1.5 billion yen debt in just six years, and Iwata had turned the company around.

"Thanks to your help, we've been able to recover," said Iwata to Nintendo president Yamauchi during a visit to Nintendo.

"Will you come work for us?" was Yamauchi's reply to Iwata, who'd gained experience as a business manager. It was a difficult time; Sony was pressing in. This would be a new quest. Iwata felt it was time to return the favor Nintendo had done him, and immediately agreed.

There was another reason for his ready agreement—Iwata was only too happy for a chance to work side-by-side with a game developer he respected deeply: Shigeru Miyamoto.

Breaking the Rules: Shigeru Miyamoto

He's nominated every year for *Time* magazine's "100 Most Influential People" list. In 2007 he and then-Toyota president Katsuaki Watanabe were the only two Japanese people on it. In 2008 he was selected in a reader poll on *Time*'s website as the *most* influential person, pulling in almost two million votes in the process. He is world-famous.

He is Shigeru Miyamoto, Nintendo's senior executive.

Miyamoto's fame, surprisingly, started in America, and is more widespread abroad than it is in Japan.

It started with the arcade game craze, when the kids were all playing a game called *Donkey Kong*, and continued with a character by the name of Mario, whose history now spans more than 20 years. Miyamoto's work has since garnered him worldwide fame and recognition; he has received countless awards.

(Est. 1945)

社団
法人 日本外国特派員協会

Iwata (right) and Miyamoto fielding questions at the Japan Foreign Correspondents Club in December 2006. As a fellow creator of games, Iwata was always in pursuit of Miyamoto. [Photo © AFP/Jiji]

For example, in 2006 he was awarded the distinction of *chevalier* in the French *Légion d'honneur*, an order originally established by Napoleon Bonaparte. In 2007 British magazine *The Economist* gave him their Innovation Award in the category of consumer products. The list goes on and on.

Iwata held Miyamoto in the highest regard, and as a fellow game creator, set his sights on catching up to the master and learning his secrets. While Iwata is now technically Miyamoto's superior within the company, he is still (by his own admission) "the biggest Miyamoto fan in the world," respecting him as the man who "set down the basic grammar for videogames."

Yet as Iwata says, "It's as though the man who wrote the rules went and broke them." Indeed, as Miyamoto continues to work on such un-game-like games such as *Wii Fit*, his reputation as an innovator only grows.

Worldwide, his name is introduced with words like "legendary" and "genius," yet his roots lie in a suburb of Kyoto, among the same backyard hills you can find anywhere in Japan.

As Miyamoto, a native of the town of Sonobe (now part of Nantan City) wrote in the opening sentences for a 2001 column entitled "To All of You Who Hail From Tanba" that ran in the *Kyoto Shinbun*:

> The setting for games like *Super Mario Brothers* and *Pikmin* comes directly from mountains like Komugiyama and Tenjinyama. I scrambled around the shrines at their peaks and down their slopes, detective badge pinned to my shirt as I searched for caves...

He spent his early years covered in mud from scampering about the mountains, fishing, and poking around in caves. It was there that he formed the memories that would come to inform his games.

A small town of ten thousand-odd people just shy of an hour outside of Kyoto on the *San'in* rail line; it was there that Miyamoto was raised, attending the town's public schools.

While he was by turns mischievous and innocent as he ran

about the town, his drawings also received praise from his first grade teacher, and he grew to love drawing. By the time he entered middle school he was deeply enamored with comics and founded a "Comics Research Society" with his friends. In high school, he joined the mountaineering club and hiked Komugiyama with a backpack full of sand for training.

Miyamoto enrolled in Kanazawa Municipal Art College to pursue a career in industrial design, which he felt would mesh well with his fondness for plastic models, crafting, and toys as well as drawing and sculpting.

It was around this time that he learned music. He practiced guitar on his own, forming a band with some friends. Experiencing the joy of creating music with other people—no matter how clumsy— ultimately found expression in *Wii Music*, a game that let even the rankest amateur join a jam session with a wave of the Wii Remote.

Thanks to his free-spirited upbringing, when Miyamoto approached graduation he decided it would be a lot of fun to work at this toy company based in Kyoto and went for an interview.

At the time, Nintendo was moving beyond card games. To break into the videogame market, Nintendo needed people with expertise in art and industrial design.

So it was that Miyamoto came to work for Nintendo in 1977, at the age of 24. He was the first designer the company ever hired, though his work began with nothing but poster and package design. Four years later came a turning point—and the beginning of a legend.

It wasn't as though Miyamoto had originally come to work for Nintendo to do videogames; he was not a programmer like Iwata. What first distinguished him as a game creator was a 1981 arcade game meant for export to the US.

At the time, videogame arcades were sweeping Japan, spurred on by the success of Taito's *Space Invaders* game. Nintendo wanted a share of this business and was well into the development of their own arcade game. Their Game & Watch series of portable electronic games, introduced in 1980, was meeting with success, and Nintendo devoted its business resources to developing two arcade machines.

Nintendo of America (NOA) was incorporated in 1980 to facilitate expansion abroad. However, a major part of this push, a game called *Radar Scope*, went largely unsold.

In response to the request from NOA to develop a new game that could run on the existing *Radar Scope* cabinet and hardware, the home office decided to create a game based on one of their Game & Watch titles.

With Game & Watch's ongoing success, there was no way they could form a new development team just to make up for an overstock situation in America. In searching for their salvation, what came up was a game already in development as a new title for the Game & Watch series: *Popeye*.

Popeye—based on the American cartoon—would have name recognition. If they could load it onto the excess *Radar Scope* cabinets, they would have no trouble selling them, the logic went. It was onto this project that Miyamoto's boss invited him.

However, licensing problems froze the project in its tracks— Nintendo was not allowed to use the likeness of Popeye or any of the related characters in the game, even though development of the gameplay and levels was proceeding well. They would have to create alternate characters. Miyamoto-the-artist's day had finally come.

Instead of Popeye, Miyamoto created "Mario." In Olive Oyl's place was "Princess Peach," and instead of Bluto, there would be "Donkey Kong." He proposed new ideas like "Donkey Kong throws barrels" and "Mario jumps to evade them," which were added. It was his debut as a game creator.

Miyamoto designed the Mario character with an outfit that would fit with the game's setting, which was a construction site, and added a mustache, which would be discernible even with the coarse graphics. Originally he just called the character "the ol' man," but when the game was shown to a Nintendo of America employee, he claimed the character looked just like a colleague named "Mario." The rest is history.

Footsteps: Shigeru Miyamoto

TIME	EVENT
Nov. 16, 1952 (age 0)	Born in town of Sonobe (today Nantan city), Kyoto prefecture.
1965 (age 12)	Enters Sonobe Township Middle School. Obsessed with drawing comics, forms "Comics Research Society."
April 1977 (age 24)	After majoring in industrial design at Kanazawa Municipal Art College, enters Nintendo.
1980 (age 27)	Involved in development of arcade game *Donkey Kong*, creates Mario.
1984 (age 31)	Promoted to Section Head, Entertainment Analysis and Development. Develops *Super Mario Bros.* for the NES.
1996 (age 43)	Promoted to Manager when EAD is upgraded from department to division.
1998 (age 45)	Promoted to General Manager of EAD. Hands-on supervision of game development for the NINTENDO64.
June 2000 (age 47)	Appointed to board together with Iwata, who has joined mid-career. Retains post as General Manager of EAD.
May 2002 (age 49)	Appointed senior executive. Hands-on supervision of game development for the GameCube.

Unlike its predecessor, *Donkey Kong* did not go unsold. Far from it—orders poured in. It was a huge hit, ultimately selling over 60,000 units. Miyamoto had discovered the joy of game design. It was the beginning of a flood of popular games from the designer, and his ascent to worldwide recognition.

A Look Over the Shoulder

San Francisco, March 2007. Two years earlier, Iwata had delivered the keynote address at the Game Developers Conference; this year the task fell to Miyamoto. He started by talking about a uniquely Miyamoto-esque index for measuring the success of Nintendo's strategy to broaden gaming's appeal: the Wife-o-meter.

Miyamoto's wife had never had any interest in videogames. But one day, he spied her watching their daughter play *The Legend of Zelda: The Ocarina of Time*. Then he wondered—could he get his wife to play? He gave her *Animal Crossing*, a game where the object is simply to have fun living in a village full of animals. "There aren't any enemies in this one," he told her—and she picked up the controller and played.

When the DS came out, she enjoyed playing *Nintendogs*. Her attitude toward videogames was changing. When the Wii came out, she turned it on of her own accord and used the Mii character creator to make caricatures of her family and friends, happily showing them off.

"When I saw my wife having fun with the Mii creator, it meant we'd taken a step forward in game design. Once she comes up with a unique game of her own, I'll be able to retire."

Laughter echoed through the meeting hall.

Miyamoto's ideas were largely responsible for the side-scrolling *Super Mario* series of games, which took their cues from the places he'd played as a child. The same goes for *Zelda*, another series with worldwide appeal.

From the characters to the level design, story, and gameplay, Miyamoto had a hand in it all. His ability to design game after hit game hasn't declined even now that he's an executive.

He continues to produce not only titles like *Mario* and *Zelda*, which set down the grammar of videogames, but also titles like *Animal Crossing* and *Nintendogs*, which flaunt that same grammar.

Yet Miyamoto is not doing anything special. He simply lives and plays for the fun of it, and when he finds a hint or an idea there in his daily life, he puts it into a game.

But he does have something that sets him apart from the average person—an insatiable inquisitiveness and a keen sense of smell.

It was 2000, and game sales had fallen off. Some said it was temporary, a side effect of the approaching turnover in console hardware generations. Others pointed to increasing cell phone use as the cause. Miyamoto disagreed.

On the train, he saw kids sending text messages to each other constantly. They were clearly enjoying themselves. As he watched them tap out rapid-fire missives on their phones' keypads as though they were playing a game, he felt a terrible jealousy.

Later he would sarcastically say to some of Nintendo's software team, "Sending text messages is way more fun for them than any game we make. If we made a game where you have to type a certain message as fast as possible and competed nationwide, that'd probably be the most fun game in Japan."

"I really was jealous of the way cell phones integrated into their lives. I knew games were going to have to do the same," says Miyamoto, who went on to make *Animal Crossing*, a game with casual communication at the heart of its design.

Iwata was not yet president, and the strategy of growing the gaming population was still in the distance. "The action games we're making are getting old," Miyamoto realized. He called for "games that satisfy just by holding them."

Without enemies to fight, without a story to follow or a goal to pursue, just lazily whiling the day away. Word of *Animal Crossing* spread especially among women in their teens and twenties, and it became a hit. At one point retailers couldn't keep it in stock.

The DS version, *Animal Crossing: Wild World*, featured casual network play, allowing players to have friends visit their village, or go on a visit themselves. In Japan it sold an astonishing 5 million copies by February 2009.

Miyamoto's keen observations on play likewise contributed significantly to the success of the Wii.

In the middle of 2005, with the development of the Wii Remote settling down, the hardware team began development on the main unit itself, and Miyamoto returned to his own "room," throwing himself into the development of the software that would make the Wii a success. He was the general manager of Analysis and Development—which within the company at large was known as the "Jokai" (from the kanji characters used to write "analysis" and "development") but was simply "The Room" to its members, a gang of pros Miyamoto had nurtured.

In the Room, they'd already started work on the games that had to launch with the Wii, but the development tracks kept multiplying, and there was no order. Miyamoto sketched out an informal diagram on a single sheet of paper. It was the grand design for the software that would support the Wii at its launch, including the ways in which each game would connect with the main unit's functions.

There was a "Party Pack," which included games that would let the whole family enjoy the Wii's new intuitive controls, and a "Sports Pack" that included games based on a variety of sports.

By the time the system launched, those ideas would become the games *Wii Sports* and *Wii Play*. But Miyamoto's note included another idea—the "Health Pack." It would become *Wii Fit*.

Its inspiration was a bathroom scale.

After Miyamoto turned 40, he started a diet and began attending a swim class. He'd also been experiencing some back pain, possibly due to the large amount of time he spent sitting. As he continued to swim, his weight naturally dropped. That was when he first realized that, hey, getting in shape can be kind of fun.

Miyamoto had always been something of a bad boy. The straight and narrow had never really suited him, but now he found himself quitting smoking and pachinko in favor of diet and exercise.

However, after a while his weight started creeping back toward its old level. He started weighing himself every day, putting a chart in the bathroom and graphing even minute fluctuations. It was the ritualized habit of weighing himself before his daily bath that led him to the realization that the routine had become fun. It was 2004, before even the DS was released.

A year passed as he continued to graph his weight before he finally began a game project based around the ideas of weighing yourself and getting in shape.

The project crystallized into the Health Pack, a strategic piece of Wii software. It would lead users through yoga and balance games. It came bundled with the Wii Balance Board, a scale that could measure both weight and center of gravity—for the first time, weighing yourself became a game.

Progression of *Wii Fit* Sales: Japan, US, and Europe

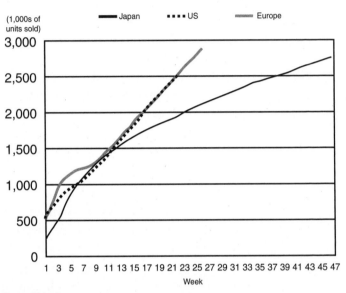

Source: Nintendo

Wii Fit went on sale in Japan in December 2007, debuting internationally in April and May 2008. Like *Brain Age* for the DS, *Wii Fit* became a powerful force behind Wii console sales.

By late December 2008, *Wii Fit* had sold roughly 14 million units worldwide. According to videogame magazine giant Enterbrain, Inc., between July and September 2008, *Wii Fit* was the second best-selling game in Japan, the US, and the UK. The world had embraced Miyamoto's hobby.

Nintendo has an official retail store in New York City's Rockefeller Center. In October 2008, six months after *Wii Fit*'s release in the US and at the height of the credit crisis, dozens of people still lined up in front of the store before it opened, and the scene of customers running through the doors and back to the registers became a daily occurrence.

Nearly all of them were trying to get *Wii Fit*, and one out of every three or four was buying a Wii console to go with it. Throughout

2008 Nintendo had been forced to increase production to 2.4 million units a month, up 33% from the previous year.

It's a good example of the success that comes from Miyamoto's tireless search for play, but that is not where his strength ends. Iwata calls Miyamoto's technique "a look over the shoulder."

When creating a game, Miyamoto will occasionally find employees from, say, general affairs who aren't gamers and put a controller in their hands, looking over their shoulder and watching them play without saying anything. By doing so, he can identify places to improve. "That part's too difficult." "They don't seem to be noticing that mechanism," and so on.

In his own words: "We're always trying to make games that will make people play for the first time, so the feedback we get from people that are already really into games isn't enough, sometimes."

The world-famous Miyamoto had always been listening to non-gamers even before that was Nintendo's corporate strategy. No matter how famous or successful he became, it was never "my way or the highway" for him; if "normal people" didn't get something about his game, then it was his fault and he'd get it fixed.

That "look over the shoulder" is a potent weapon.

Miyamoto's quest for sniffing out the play—the *fun*—of life has given rise to extraordinary innovation. He begins with those innovations, then polishes them earnestly, even naively, until everyone can enjoy them.

The process is almost ascetic.

Flipping the Table

In mid-2006, just shy of half a year before the introduction of the Wii, Nintendo's best game development team received a major shock.

The first *Legend of Zelda* game had been introduced in 1986, and since then the action role-playing (RPG) series had gone on to sell some 45 million copies in total worldwide. Nintendo EAD was working at a fever pitch to finish the latest entry in the series, *The Legend of Zelda: Twilight Princess*.

Zelda had been promised to debut along with the Wii itself, and like it or not, expectations for the game were rising all over the world. It had been originally slated to ship around the end of 2005, so delaying it further was impossible. Translation of the game from Japanese into the languages of various other markets had already started.

It was upon that cornered, panicking development team that Miyamoto came calling to deliver the following death knell: "So about that first village—one day is too short. Let's make it three."

Before the game's protagonist, Link, goes on his grand adventure, he stays in a village, during which the story's prologue plays out as the player learns how to use the game's controls. The development team had settled on Link staying in the village for a single day, and the programming for it had been completed for some time. But now Miyamoto was telling them to change that.

It was not a simple matter of extending the amount of time Link spent in the village. In order to have players feel comfortable entering the world of *Zelda* with the Wii's new controller, he felt the starting village was lacking a beat or two. The number of items would rise, and the characters' animations and spoken lines would change. Naturally the village's map data would also have to be transformed.

Development on the game was approaching its final stages, and the team was working overtime day after day to hone and refine the final product. Miyamoto's order was their worst nightmare. It was like he'd walked in and flipped the table over. Still, the development team hurried to implement the changes, informing the overseas branches, "We're altering the entire starting village. Halt translation."

After Miyamoto left the front lines of development and dedicated himself to a role as general producer, his "flipping the table" became famous throughout the company, even overseas.

Flipping the table on the *Zelda* team just as they were coming up against their deadline must have seemed inexcusable from their perspective. However, while they were half-terrified, there was also some measure of gratitude. Miyamoto did not simply come in and upend their work; he always gave them directions on how to improve it—setting the bowls and chopsticks back on the table in a new arrangement, so to speak. His input was sound, and in the end the team appreciated it.

His "three-day plan" for the starting village in the new *Zelda* game was no exception.

In the behind-the-scenes information for the game as presented on Nintendo's web site, one staffer recalls: "The things we changed made it easier to get accustomed to the Wii Remote, but that wasn't all—it also got a lot easier to get sucked into the world of *Zelda*. In the end, I'm really glad we had to change it."

And the *Zelda* team got off easy. They managed to finish the game and make their ship date. Sometimes Miyamoto's implacable hammer came down hard enough to outright cancel a project.

Iwata had experienced it personally.

In 1991, as HAL Laboratory's debt increased and they teetered on the edge of ruin, Iwata (then serving on HAL's board of directors) bet the company on a single game. It was called *Tinkle Popo*. It was created by an up-and-coming designer at HAL, Masahiro Sakurai, and Iwata had planned not to publish it under Nintendo's name the way a typical second-party title was, instead selling it as a HAL game—he wanted it to be the game that turned the company around.

However, when *Tinkle Popo*—which had already been publicly announced as going on sale in late January 1991—caught Miyamoto's eye toward the end of 1990, he forced them to halt development on it, even though a respectable 26,000 copies had already been preordered.

Of course, Miyamoto was not being malicious. When he saw the game, he simply decided it would be a waste not to make it the best game it could be. He also believed that the game would sell better if Nintendo and not HAL published it.

The protagonist's name was changed from "Popopo" to "Kirby," and one year and three months later, the game was reborn, released to the world as *Kirby's Dream Land*. It was HAL's biggest hit since the company's founding, and a significant factor in its turnaround.

The pre-orders were canceled, and the game went on sale after having been postponed for over a year. The results were good, but the results were not why Miyamoto had done what he did. It was simply that he couldn't stand putting out product with which he wasn't happy.

Which is why he'll polish one for years, if he has to, until it satisfies him.

For example, the Mii Channel, a key part of the Wii's charm, was 20 years in the making. For Miyamoto, shelving an idea does not mean throwing it away. Those huge storehouses are full of precious treasure that will someday see the light of day.

The Mii Channel allows users to create caricatured avatars by building faces from a selection of facial contours, eyes, eyebrows, noses, mouths, and hairstyles. As part of the Wii Menu, it comes with every Wii. The avatars—"Miis"—created within the Mii Channel can be used as characters in games like *Wii Sports* and *Wii Fit*.

Iwata takes any chance to explain that the Mii Channel is "the result of Miyamoto persistently thinking about it for nearly 20 years."

"It'd be neat if you could put yourself in a game."

The first time the idea occurred to Miyamoto was in 1986, with the release of the Famicom Disk System, a floppy disk peripheral for the Famicom. But when they created a prototype caricature-creation program for the Disk System, they "didn't know what to do with the characters it made," so the project was canceled.

He buried the idea of a caricature program for a while, but it came up again in 2000, this time as a game for the Nintendo 64 DD, a short-lived peripheral for the 64 that used magnetic disks instead of cartridges. The game was called *Talent Studio*, and allowed players to apply faces to simple 3-D models, then animate them to create movies. But since it was software for the 64 DD—sold only in Japan, and in very limited quantities—it was highly experimental. The 64 DD was gone within a year, unmourned.

But Miyamoto didn't give up on the idea. At E3 2002, he revealed the development of a GameCube game called *Stage Debut*, which again prominently featured caricature creation—this time with pictures taken with a camera that attached to the Game Boy Advance, which were then transferred to the GameCube. Going into 2004, it was renamed *Ningen Kopii Manebito* ("Human Copy Lookalike") and as production proceeded, the title was even trademarked.

But in the end there was still no clear idea of what players would *do* with their creatures, so it was shelved once again. But still Miyamoto didn't give up, and when he sketched out the diagram for the game lineup that would launch with the Wii, he was bent on having his revenge.

The project that resulted in the characters in games like *Wii Sports* being player-created caricatures started just before the release of the Wii. It was spearheaded by Miyamoto and developed by the analysis and design division, and was called "Kokeshi."

Completely removed from Miyamoto and his Kokeshi project was another team, working on a piece of caricature software for the DS. When Iwata learned about this, and knowing of Miyamoto's enthusiasm for caricature, he told Miyamoto right away about the DS project. Miyamoto took the bait.

"I think it'll be good for you guys, do you want to come work with us? We'll put our best director on it, and it'll be an amazing team," Miyamoto offered the DS caricature team—and with that, they were part of the Kokeshi project. The ideas Miyamoto had had for 20 years finally came to fruition with the Mii Channel.

No matter how many tables he flips, in the end Miyamoto will bring place settings from other tables to perfect the final product. Iwata explains Miyamoto's eccentricity this way:

"Looking at Miyamoto, I'm always impressed. He's got the ability to just out of nowhere say, 'Hey, this isn't very tasty, but if you combine it with this it's delicious,' and bring together totally unrelated projects. He takes something that looks like it's going to waste and turns it into a meal."

As Analysis and Development was coming close to finishing *Wii Fit*,

Miyamoto agonized over the game's aerobic exercise options.

A course of step aerobics set to music, and a hula hoop activity—both using the Wii Balance Board—had been decided, but it wasn't enough. For Miyamoto, who was continuing his swimming and now gym visits, there needed to be something that could really work up a sweat.

Around the same time, Miyamoto would visit the *Wii Sports* team to see how their experiments were going.

They were working on the sequel to *Wii Sports* and were groping around for new games to include. At the time, they were testing out a prototype of a jogging game. The Wii Remote included motion-sensing accelerometers, so a player could put the remote in their pocket, and it would be able to sense the count and pace of the strides they took. "I can use this," Miyamoto thought, then spoke up: "We don't know if we're doing *Wii Sports 2* yet, so let me use this for *Wii Fit*. Oh, and lend me the programmer, too."

Miyamoto himself had made a rule, during the development of *Wii Fit*, that all of the activities had to use the Wii Balance Board. He changed his own rule just to include jogging, which didn't use the Balance Board at all—but instead a Wii Remote, in the pocket.

Staying flexible and adaptable in order to make fun games, games that people will find satisfying—that's the Miyamoto way. Anything goes, even if he has to flip a few tables, break his own rules, or snatch ideas and people from other projects.

This culture—call it "Miyamotoism"—has completely infused Analysis and Development. It's what lets members of shelved or postponed projects keep moving forward without losing morale.

In October 2008, at a corporate strategy briefing, after reminiscing about Miyamoto's tenacity, Iwata summed it up this way: "It's important to think long and persistently, and the accumulation of long, careful thought is what gives rise to a hit, is what I think it comes down to."

Creating prototypes, discarding them, creating more. Miyamoto's table-flipping is just a frank, honest expression of his attitude toward games. That spirit is what built a regime that discards bad games and strives to give the world only the very best.

"Miyamotoism"—Bringing Down the Walls

The year 2004, with Iwata as president of Nintendo, saw the company effect a massive internal reorganization, including merging the storied research and development sections one and two with the relatively new planning and development division.

Broadly speaking, hardware sections were reorganized into the Integrated Research and Development Division (for home consoles) and the Technology and Engineering Division (for portables), while software resources were divided into the Entertainment Analysis and Development Division (for internal software projects) and the Software Planning Development Division (for cooperating with developers outside the company).

Iwata wanted to bring down the walls that separated the different sections of the company and increase opportunities for collaboration. His ultimate goal: the spread of "Miyamotoism."

Sectionalism within Nintendo was traditionally strong, but it had also drawn out individuality and originality. Former president Yamauchi had adopted a policy of establishing development positions to suit specific individuals.

In 1979, Yamauchi split the research and development department. Research and Development 1 (R&D 1) was headed by Gunpei Yokoi, creator of the Ultra Hand (a toy with a scissor-action extending gripper) and the Ray Gun (predecessor to the NES's Zapper Gun), and R&D 2 would be led by Masayuki Uemura, who had transferred from Sharp. The two groups had an ongoing rivalry.

R&D 1 focused mainly on portable devices like the Game & Watch series and the Game Boy, while R&D 2 was responsible for the development of home consoles like the NES and SNES. Both departments also produced games.

In 1984, Yamauchi called Miyamoto into his office, and gave the designer his own group, Nintendo Entertainment Analysis and Development (EAD) that would specialize in game software. Miyamoto immediately produced the huge hit that was *Super Mario Bros.*, and thereafter the Miyamoto Corps nurtured its own culture, maturing into the single largest software faction within Nintendo.

1989 saw the release of the Game Boy, with R&D 1 mostly working on software for the portable device. EAD (which in 1996 was elevated to its own division) focused on developing games for Nintendo's home consoles, though each group had projects outside its specialty.

With the release of each new hardware platform, the number of development departments would increase, and Nintendo software experienced different evolutionary paths for portable and home systems. The walls between Miyamoto's EAD division and the other software development teams were especially thick, with few examples of meaningful synergy.

Thus, starting with the newly established Planning and Development division, Iwata aimed to link them to EAD.

Brain Age, a mega-hit released in May 2005, was based on an idea Iwata brought in himself, and was completed with him at the center of development. The project had been assigned to Planning and Development.

Much of the Planning and Development division's work was carried out in cooperation with external, second-party developers. Since they specialize in titles for Nintendo's portable systems, the actual software development burden is relatively light.

Ever since *Brain Age*, Iwata—who had originally been a developer himself—used Planning and Development to ride the wave as a game creator.

He acted as producer for a variety of hit titles, unconventional projects that he started himself. There was *DS Rakubiki Jiten* ("DS Easy-lookup Dictionary"), which used handwriting recognition to look up words in English-Japanese, Japanese-English, and Japanese dictionaries. *Brain Age* had a sequel: *Brain Age 2: More Training in Minutes a Day!* There were even more explicitly educational titles, like *English Training: Have Fun Improving Your Skills!*, and *Imasara Hito ni*

The Development Department at Nintendo: A History

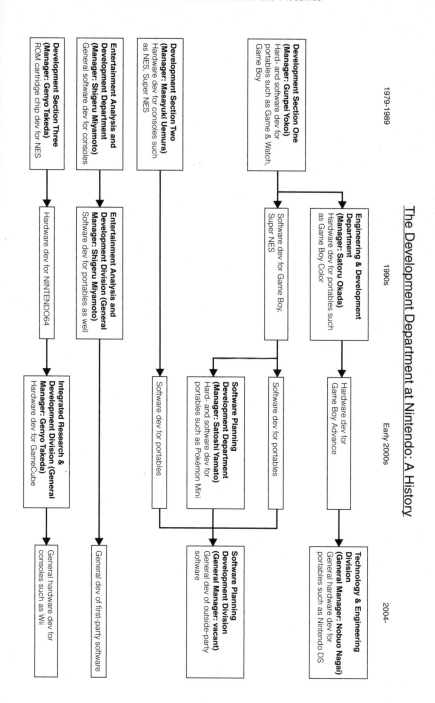

1979-1989

Development Section One (Manager: Gunpei Yokoi)
Hard- and software dev for portables such as Game & Watch, Game Boy

Development Section Two (Manager: Masayuki Uemura)
Hardware dev for consoles such as NES, Super NES

Entertainment Analysis and Development Department (Manager: Shigeru Miyamoto)
General software dev for consoles

Development Section Three (Manager: Genyo Takeda)
ROM cartridge chip dev for NES

1990s

Engineering & Development Department (Manager: Satoru Okada)
Hardware dev for portables such as Game Boy Color

Software dev for Game Boy, Super NES

Entertainment Analysis and Development Division (General Manager: Shigeru Miyamoto)
Software dev for portables as well

Hardware dev for NINTENDO64

Early 2000s

Hardware dev for Game Boy Advance

Software dev for portables

Software Planning Development Department (Manager: Satoshi Yamato)
Hard- and software dev for portables such as Pokémon Mini

Software dev for portables

Integrated Research & Development Division (General Manager: Genyo Takeda)
Hardware dev for GameCube

2004-

Technology & Engineering Division (General Manager: Nobuo Nagai)
General hardware dev for portables such as Nintendo DS

Software Planning Development Division (General Manager: vacant)
General dev of outside-party software

General dev of first-party software

General hardware dev for consoles such as Wii

Kikenai Otona no Joshikiryoku Training DS ("I'm too old not to know this stuff! Adult Common Sense Training DS").

But Iwata's success with these games came only because he had the backing of Miyamoto, whom he'd respected for so long.

"The programmer that Mr. Miyamoto sent over from his division worked on *Brain Age* as the director. His instincts were really great, and starting with his first prototype for the calculations game, the controls felt just spot-on. We got very lucky."

The director that Iwata spoke so highly of is Koichi Kawamoto, who'd had the ABCs of game design beaten into him by Miyamoto himself. Before he started on the *Brain Age* project, Iwata, having seen Dr. Kawashima's *Train Your Brain* book, went to Miyamoto. "This would be really fun, and I think it's a perfect fit for the DS," he explained. Miyamoto agreed—"I think you should do it"—and sent Kawamoto to Planning and Development by way of support for the project.

As it turned out, even before Iwata talked to Miyamoto about wanting to do *Brain Age*, Miyamoto had EAD working on a similar idea. It was called *Big Brain Academy* and was being developed for both the DS and the Wii. "Dictionaries and brain training were part of a theme I'd always wanted to try. But *Mario* and *Zelda* were always chasing me, and I could never make it happen. So when Iwata got ahead of me, I was a little jealous," said Miyamoto. But he supported Iwata's ideas, providing logistical support to Planning and Development's project. At the same time, Iwata was happy to compartmentalize and avoided squashing Miyamoto's project. He supported both projects by serving as producer for *Big Brain Academy*.

Ultimately *Big Brain Academy* was released just a month after *Brain Age*, and while it did not see the same success as the latter game, it was a million-seller in its own right, tallying over 1.6 million copies in Japan. The simultaneous success of both games was the result of Iwata serving as a control tower for all Nintendo to let Miyamotoism thrive.

Software development that crosses departmental boundaries has grown to encompass the company.

Otona no DS Kao Training ("DS Face Training for Adults"), released in August 2007, was created by a cross-departmental team that included non-developers like administration and sales people.

Starting in 2005, Iwata started the "User Expansion Project," bringing members in from divisions throughout the company. In 2006, the second project began with the participation of employees that usually had nothing to do with development. They had total discretion, from conception to commercial realization.

Face Training aimed to take "facening," a form of cosmetic exercise in which facial tone is improved by strengthening muscles, and turn it into a game that would make it easy for anyone to practice daily. The idea came from a woman member whose normal job was in network management; it occurred to her when she was massaging her face in the bathroom of her parents' house.

The team took that idea and started to work out the project. The key to turning it into a shipping product was a technology called "face-sensing engine," which could analyze the features of a person's face and understand their expression. By using this technology, the software could process data from the camera that would ship with the game, and overlay instructional animations on top of the images of the user's face.

"I made sure to send over someone who could provide nimble technical support, who could help deliver a convincing package," said Miyamoto.

Just as he says, it was a member of EAD that suggested the addition of image recognition technology. Before the idea of facening came up, the engineer in question had attended technology exhibitions relevant to the problem, and the questions that engineer had asked there were now paying off.

Naturally, Iwata's push for more intra-company collaboration extended to hardware development as well. As mentioned earlier, Miyamoto was deeply involved with the creation of both the DS and the Wii, with many former and current members of EAD participating in the development of software aspects like main unit functions.

For example, Kawamoto, who'd been sent from EAD to Planning and Development to create *Brain Age* and *Brain Age 2*, also acted as director for several core Wii Menu components—the Photo Channel, the Forecast Channel, and the News Channel.

Nintendo has always had both hardware and software developers living under the same roof, so cooperation had always been possible. However, Miyamoto says that it wasn't until Iwata took the helm and began development of the DS that such cooperation actually happened. "Collaboration between the hardware teams and software teams became much stronger once we started to do the DS. I'd always thought of that as a strength of ours, but it was really with the DS that the company started to move. We saw good results, like sample programs on test hardware that were really persuasive, or getting a quick sense of what the finished product would be like. We wanted to have the same success with the Wii, so programmers from my division were involved in hardware development from a very early stage."

Despite both being hardware, the portable and home console departments had been distinct, with very little collaboration between the two. But that also changed, says Iwata. "Portable and home developers can easily tend to get competitive with each other. But these last few years they've stopped designing for just their fields. We're getting a set-up where both portable and home divisions are working more and more within Nintendo's grand design."

While competing against deeply global players, Nintendo created the DS and the Wii, both of which were massive hits, and published a series of million-selling games to ensure continuing hardware sales. Doing so took not only gaming ideas and passion, but also plain old institutional reorganization.

And the man at the helm of all of this is Iwata. Without his brilliant management, the story of Nintendo's success would simply not exist.

Interview with the Outsider President

Imagine, for a moment, that the company you work for has a new president. Presumably this new president would at least give some kind of company-wide address. But if you're not on the board of directors, you'd probably have no idea if or when you'd get to converse with him or her. It would be even less likely if you were part of a global company with thousands of employees.

The first thing Iwata did in 2002, when he became president of a company with sales of 550 billion yen, net profits of 100 billion yen, and which employed over 3,000 people, was meet face-to-face with those employees. He had individual interviews with all 40 department heads, and met one-on-one with the 150 people in the development group for which he was responsible.

Iwata was the first president in Nintendo's long history to come from outside the founding family. Not only that, he was not a "Nintendo native"—he hadn't been hired straight out of school, but instead had only just come to the company in 2000.

Just because the previous president Yamauchi had handpicked Iwata for the job, there was no guarantee that the Nintendo lifers on the board of directors and in the company would listen to him, a fact of which Iwata himself was fully aware. "There was no way it was going to be as easy as having the president fire off a single order to have everybody heading in the same direction, believing in this new future. Naturally a lot of people would think, 'So he says, but are we sure?'"

Yet within four years, his vision had permeated every corner of the company. How?

"I explained why Nintendo had to move in this direction many, many times. In the process, some aspect of what I was saying would come true, and then one or two more people would be on board, and it went like that until it sank in company-wide. It probably just came down to me saying the same thing over and over again," says Iwata.

He makes it sound simple, but behind the success lies a persistent, continuous effort that doesn't come easily to the average business leader.

What changed from the Yamauchi era? Miyamoto, a 30-year veteran of Nintendo, puts it this way: "In a sense, Nintendo's history had always been dictated by the single person at the top, and there were aspects of that tendency that were rather stuffy. But Iwata coming in with his outsider's perspective improved the ventilation, so to speak, and I get the feeling that the employees' understanding of management's policies became much deeper thanks to that."

During the Yamauchi years, there were only a handful of personnel that could talk directly to the president. "It was just Mr. Yamauchi's personality; he wasn't being high and mighty or anything," says Miyamoto. But in any case, the fact remained that access to the president was limited.

Even chances to hear the president speak were rare, coming but once a year and in a lecture-like format. But the Iwata era changed that; the president himself would deliver slide presentations to either a group of developers or the entire company, frequently explaining business conditions and objectives.

It went past explanation. Iwata had direct conversations with staff, continuing the practice of individual interviews he'd started at his previous job as president of Hal Laboratory.

Iwata was 42, young, for a company president. He was a former game programmer, and even now he assumes direct control over game production. Compared to Yamauchi, his perspective was significantly closer to his staff's.

He constantly put questions to employee after employee. What did you study in college? What drew you to Nintendo? What have you done here so far? What's been good, what's been bad? Individually interviewing every worker in the company was impossible, but at the very least he wanted to communicate with all the people under his direct supervision, plus the heads of every department.

By doing so, he hoped to convey his sense of crisis regarding the future of the gaming industry and explain why the need to expand the gamer population was so urgent. If they resisted, he allowed them to do as they wished, saying, "Okay, try that." Iwata believes that "creators only improve themselves by taking risks."

Even as he was betting the company on the DS and Wii, Iwata attempted face-to-face communication with rank-and-file employees. In 2006, he even started doing public interviews.

In September 2006, a strange article suddenly appeared on the Nintendo website. The title was "The President Asks: About the Wii Project." Iwata was the interviewer, with members of the development staff as his subjects.

The series of seven articles began with "Wii Hardware" and concluded the day before the release of the console on December 1.

The volume of information is overwhelming—you could stay up all night reading the articles, with easily ten hours' worth of interviews behind them. Yet it was just the tip of the iceberg.

Since then, the "Asks" series has continued to make public Iwata's interviews with a wide variety of developers, telling the development stories of everything from DS and Wii games to new peripherals to the latest version of the DS, the DSi.

In May 2007, he started the series "The President Asks: About Working at Nintendo," where he interviewed mainly younger employees about their hopes and experiences in an effort to introduce the work environment at Nintendo to those who hoped to join their ranks.

By November 2008 the series had grown to 27 installments, not counting the extra episode that featured Iwata himself as the subject. Over 120 staff members have appeared so far, from veterans like Miyamoto and *Zelda* director Eiji Aonuma, all the way down to relative newcomers to Nintendo, young employees of only a few years' experience who'd never spoken directly to Iwata before.

When the series began, Iwata explained in it why he himself was doing the interviews:

> To put it simply, it's because I thought the current structure of Nintendo makes it possible. As the president, I am involved in approving every aspect of the Wii's development, which

makes me the perfect person to objectively look at it and explain to our customers, "This is how the Wii was made."

Conveying the thinking of the developers to the public was certainly a primary goal. However, a careful reading of the interviews leaves one with the distinct impression that Iwata's true aim with the "Asks" series was deepening his own communication with his developers.

In the episode coinciding with the October 2008 launch of *Style Savvy* (a fashion game for the DS), Iwata began with the routine introductions then continued:

> Ito's real job is providing technical support for all the different software groups in Software Planning Development. Tajima was originally in Yamagami's group, and Hattori still is, but it was a little unusual to have Ito, who isn't in Yamagami's group, involved.

His perfect grasp of the relationships between the various staff members involved with the game would be surprising even in a seasoned interviewer. It also has a raw quality, as though he's not talking to consumers but rather to the staff.

"So, Koyama, it's been just a year since you came to Nintendo. What did you do before that, and what made you decide to join Nintendo?" "You were a tech expert for sales. Is that experience helping you now?"

The series of interviews on the employment section of the website unfold like real conversations, which—given their length and depth— are nigh-soaked in Iwata's dedication to good communication with his staff. It could be said that precisely because of that dedication, the rest of the company united behind him and believed in his vision.

There is still another tool Iwata used to deepen communication. It, too, is something that didn't exist during the Yamauchi era.

Adding Science to Tradition

"So, while our midyear results show a favorable trend, how will the cascading worldwide credit crises and the changes they're wreaking in the business environment affect the game marketplace? I can't help but think that's the question on all your minds..."

October 31, 2008, Tokyo's Toranomon Hotel. At the midyear financial results meeting, Iwata himself introduced the issue that was clearly on the minds of the analysts and journalists assembled there before they could raise it in the Q-and-A session.

At the same time, he brought up a slide on the giant screen behind him. It was titled "United States Home Console Sales Figures" and showed a graph of the Wii's sales rising high above the PS3 and Xbox 360's. He continued:

"We collect sales data for our own products weekly. Every week I take a careful look at those reports, and so far I see no danger of them slowing."

He went on, showing graphs of portable sales in the US, then home console and portable sales in Europe. "In an environment where retailers are expecting sales to drop in a variety of areas, the reality is that they're telling us, 'We don't have enough of your product. Send more.'"

Iwata's presentations are an onslaught of graphs, diagrams, and figures.

Using large amounts of data collected both internally and from outside research organs, he develops his thesis with logic and rhythm. Nintendo's financial results meeting handouts probably have more graphs than any other publicly traded company.

The day he denied the effects of the recession on Nintendo was the midyear financial results meeting, so he only needed to discuss reports through the end of September. But Iwata said, "We can't make any assurances just using the data through September. I'm well aware that there's the view that the market has changed in October." He thus made sure to reinforce his message with data from just the previous week that had come in from Nintendo's US offices.

87

In this presentation on the upcoming challenges Iwata expected Nintendo to face, he preemptively posed a variety of hypothetical questions—"Perhaps third-party games aren't selling well on Nintendo hardware?" "Isn't domestic performance an indicator for international trends?" "Won't the DS and Wii be peaking this year?"—using hard data and logic to refute each one.

Iwata is naturally skilled at logical explanation. His demeanor is friendly and open, and he always listens carefully to others before giving his view. He's good enough at the game that his audiences are nearly ready to agree with him on the basis of his communication skills alone, but backing his case with hard data lends it extra persuasive power.

And this weapon of Iwata's, the spice called data, sees just as much use in his communication within the company.

What changed in the Iwata era? According to Takeda, general manager of Nintendo's engineering, "the soul of the company didn't change, but once Iwata took over, we saw more science."

Miyamoto agrees. "Yamauchi made predictions based on uncanny intuition and experience. By contrast, Iwata searches for useful new elements that might be scientifically unearthed in things that experience has rejected, building up hypotheses one by one and trying to find support for them. If he finds that support, it'll get folded into his strategy. Intuition turning into conviction enables him to act and makes it easier for him to convince others."

It must be said that what Iwata is favoring isn't marketing per se. What marketing does is take a snapshot of current needs. Developing products based on those needs means releasing a product geared to the past rather than seizing the future. That goes against the grain of Iwata's thinking.

Instead, what Iwata favors is data. They allow him to back up hypotheses about what is happening and to say what he wants to say with thoroughness. The net he casts to collect that data is a wide one indeed.

The year after Iwata became president, in October 2003, Nintendo launched its "Club Nintendo" site. Registration was free of charge and there were no annual fees. Members could earn points by purchasing Nintendo hardware and games and spend them on special Nintendo merchandise that weren't commercially available.

Not unlike many airlines' frequent flyer programs, members whose yearly point totals exceeded a certain amount would qualify for "gold" or "platinum" memberships that came with special privileges. In 2007, the incentive offered to high-level members included a special controller for the Wii that was modeled after the old SNES controllers.

In addition to simple purchases, points could be earned by preordering products and completing customer surveys. Club Nintendo both encouraged sales and helped measure customer satisfaction. The data gathered through this system significantly impacted strategy proposals and commonly appeared in presentations both within and without the company.

The materials for Iwata's presentations don't stop there. An external research firm was hired to conduct a large-scale face-to-face survey. Domestically, 3,000 samples were obtained in Tokyo and Osaka, and similar efforts have been underway abroad, in the US, the UK, Germany, and France.

The graph of age and gender distribution among DS and Wii users—which Iwata likes to use to assess Nintendo's appeal-broadening strategy—was generated using the data from these face-to-face surveys.

The Wii Menu itself features a function where users can provide feedback about the Wii games they have played, and the data gained this way even informed decisions about how to improve the system. For example, some users were running out of memory space, so the ability to store downloaded software on an external SD card was added.

Showing a good grasp of almost every project within his company, occasionally taking personal charge of one or the other, all while dealing with investors and the media, Iwata probably is the busiest company president in Japan as he manages the helm with the world as his stage. Yet he devotes time to internal communication, saying the same things over and over again until his employees are convinced, not forgetting to take a scientific approach to increase his persuasiveness.

"In my view I've truly made Nintendo's values my own, and I don't think much has changed. I certainly have no intention of rejecting how Yamauchi did things; I respect it. But I do think, 'Hey, there's this thing called the internet now,' and about how to keep Nintendo's values alive in a new environment. And I'm an outsider. There's no way everyone in the company should listen to my whim the way they did with the previous president with his fifty years of experience. So I knew I had to be very, very thorough."

Iwata's work goes well beyond "thorough." It was with ascetic commitment that he pursued the strategy of broadening gaming's appeal. His results more than speak for themselves, and he has certainly earned his place.

Yet he insists he's merely been fortunate.

"As far as results go, I think things have gone very well. But without the opportune moment, I don't think I could do the same, and without the traditional culture and philosophy of Nintendo, I couldn't do it, either."

The "culture and philosophy of Nintendo" that Iwata touts so is a jewel of know-how that the company assembled over many years as it survived in the harsh business of amusement, where there is only heaven and hell and nothing in between.

4

Manufacturing Smiles: A Philosophy

"Being original and flexible—in a sense, that's Nintendo's mission statement. [...] Also, you have to love making people happy. To put it another way, you like to service."

—Iwata

Amusement Fundamentalism

If you entered a McDonald's in Setagaya ward, Tokyo, in June 2008, you would have seen a sign hanging from the ceiling that said "DS at M."

The "M" was the famous golden arches of McDonald's. Sitting down, you'd notice a similar sticker stuck on one of the tables. At the table is a youngster with a DS stylus in their right hand, cramming a hamburger into their mouth with their left. You'd think they're playing a videogame—but you'd be wrong.

On the DS's screen is a menu with items like "Cheeseburger" and "Premium Blend Iced Coffee." There might be coupons good for discounts, or even PR for being a proud sponsor of the Beijing Olympics. You can't actually make an order, but it's such an effective information terminal, you'd be forgiven for thinking that all you have to do is tap an item to have it brought right to your table.

Looking at the post-DS Nintendo—which is to say, Nintendo since the advent of Iwata—it's easy to wonder just what kind of business they're supposed to be.

Taking games into the mainstream meant expanding beyond the categories of traditional game genres into new ways to play. Broadening the scope of their business into more and more of everyday life was part and parcel of that, creating new activities for their consoles that have nothing to do with games.

In May 2008, Nintendo unveiled their "Nintendo Spot" information service, in cooperation with McDonald's and the Tsukuba Express train line.

Nintendo Spot access points were installed at select McDonald's locations in Tokyo (21 in Tokyo), and at all 20 station on the Tsukuba Express between Akihabara and Tsukuba, as well as on board the train itself. Users could access the wireless LAN service free of charge.

On the Tsukuba Express, the content lineup made you wonder if their real rival was the cell phone industry. News clippings with pictures were available from news agency Jiji Press, with Nippon Sports soon coming on board with sports and entertainment news. Weather forecasts and restaurant and accommodation information along the line were also online, along with content from Nippon TV variety shows like *Gyoretsu no Dekiru Houritsu Soudanjo* ("Line up for legal advice") and *Ippunkan no Fukaii Hanashi* ("Amazing one-minute stories").

Both the McDonald's and the Tsukuba Express installations were limited-time trial runs of the idea, but satisfied with the results, Nintendo renamed the service "Nintendo Zone" and began an official rollout. Starting with McDonald's locations in the Tokyo, Nagoya, and Kansai regions, they planned to steadily expand the availability of the service.

And it isn't just Japan that's seeing constant expansion of these invisible data services for the DS—they're appearing abroad, too.

In July 2007, an experimental content delivery service was installed at Safeco Field, the home stadium for the Seattle Mariners. Called "The Nintendo Fan Network," it passed its trial period and became an official service in April 2008. A paid service, it costs five dollars for a single game, or 30 dollars for ten games—but for that money, it delivers an excellent value.

The upper screen delivers a live video feed of the game, while the lower screen delivers statistics for not only the Mariners, but every Major League Baseball team. If you get hungry, you can use the DS to order a hot dog or soft drink delivered right to your seat.

There's an ongoing trivia contest that matches the progress of the game, and promotional contests with prizes like DS units signed by various Mariners.

The DS is becoming an information terminal to use in town, on the train, and at the baseball field.

Once the DS broke the 20 million unit barrier in Japan, Iwata started talking about the possibilities it opened up for public and commercial spaces.

"I think this is the first time a single platform like this—portable, accessible to everyone, capable of wireless communication and downloading new applications—has penetrated the market on this kind of scale."

When Iwata says "a single platform," he means a group of devices that can all use the same software with the same manner of handling. The number of cellular phones in Japan is obviously far beyond the number of DSs, but depending on the model their OS and internet browsing capabilities are totally different, which means content producers must consider each device separately.

But with the DS, things are far simpler. Iwata saw this and began setting up information delivery systems. The media immediately took notice, with excited headlines like "Nintendo Challenging Cell Phones and PDAs," "Nintendo Enters the Content Delivery Business." Analysts were also pleased at the potential for new revenue sources.

But the reason Iwata was getting into the content delivery business was not to expand the company's operations or to break into a new marketplace.

"President Iwata, you talked earlier about using the DS infrastructure to create new business, but could you say something about when that would start, how it would proceed, and how it would impact earnings?"

The question was put to Iwata during the Q&A session of the April 2008 financial results briefing. At the time, the plans with McDonald's and the Tsukuba Express had not yet been revealed. Iwata's response was admonishing as he tried to deal with the ballooning expectations of the reporters and analysts.

"We've been fortunate to sell 22 million DS units, but if you want to know what I'm most afraid of, it's the idea that those DS's will be put away in the closet and no longer played with."

Selling DS's was all well and good, but if people gave up playing them, or left them behind—Nintendo was horrified by the prospect. From that fear was born the "I'm glad I have a DS" project.

If they could create places where it would be handy or advantageous to carry a DS, people would always carry them, which would in turn keep the DS marketplace energetic and healthy.

What's more, according to Iwata, Nintendo was merely creating the first showcases for this concept and didn't mean to develop the DS as a data terminal.

"There's no need for Nintendo to do it all. The most important job of Nintendo's software engineers is to create a few concrete examples of ways the hardware can be used. We thought if we could build a few instances that would make many [software developers, public space administrators, and businesses] say 'hey, we could do that,' then we could get people to start to use the DS as infrastructure."

As the company's game systems began to be used for things besides games, it seemed as though the scope of their business was expanding. But Nintendo was focused on being a "game maker," and everything they did was to advance their goal of putting and keeping their game systems in the hands of as many people as they could. They were refusing to concentrate on goals other than gaming. This is true in all respects with Nintendo.

With *Brain Age* and *English Training* for the DS, they showed that game systems could be useful for training and education, and with *Wii Sports* and *Wii Fit*, they proved that games could also be good for your health.

Other corporations and organizations saw this and followed by exploiting possible uses in education and health.

In April 2009, NEC began a service for employees and their families that provides health support services using *Wii Fit*. Users can get solid advice from healthcare professionals without ever leaving home.

In the US, some hotels are beginning to install Wii units as fitness equipment. Starting in May 2008, Westin Hotel & Resorts began installing Wii units in the fitness centers at its New York locations and others, allowing guests to work up a sweat using either *Wii Fit* or *Wii Sports*.

Serious efforts are underway in the educational realm, as well.

In January 2008, Japanese educational publishing giant Benesse Corporation released the first title in its textbook-compliant *Tokutenryoku Gakushu DS* series ("High-Score Study Guide DS"), aimed at middle school students, proclaiming it to be the next generation of their correspondence curriculum.

Nintendo's products are often used within the classroom. Since September 2007, the Ministry of Education, Culture, Sports, Science and Technology has conducted trials to measure the educational potential of the DS, distributing 560 DS units, along with software, to 13 different elementary, middle and high schools for use in the classroom.

Developments like these are unimaginable with traditional games, but now the Wii goes next to the treadmill, and the DS is bound for the classroom.

Yet Nintendo is not expanding into the health industry with the goal of "making Japan and the rest of the world healthier," nor are they trying to break into the education business to "raise your kids' grades."

"Nintendo has always been ascetic about venturing outside the domain of games. It's a company that doesn't do anything extraneous. It's unthinkable for them to collect a bunch of data and go into the health business just because *Wii Fit* was so widely adopted," says Yoichi Wada, chairman of the CESA and president of Square Enix, a major gaming software firm with a long development history with Nintendo.

In reality, in addition to NEC, subsidiaries of both Hitachi and Panasonic developed health support services that used the Wii and were aimed at institutional use. Nintendo only provided software development assistance and was uninvolved with operation and sales.

Society was finding real-world applications for the once-disdained game consoles. But that was something society itself was doing, and while Nintendo was happy to cooperate, they refrained from managing such operations themselves.

As to why, Iwata explains it this way: "After all, we're an *amusement* company."

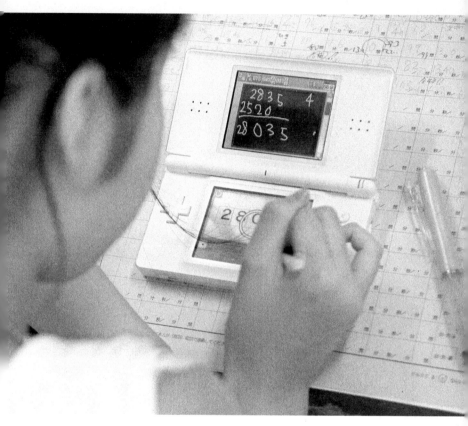

An extra session of math class enlisting the Nintendo DS Lite was held at a Tokyo middle school in August 2007. Long considered the nemesis of schoolwork, games are now helping teachers reach a digital generation. [Photo © Getty Images]

Under the banner of gamer population growth, Nintendo single-mindedly pursued a videogame revival. But even as their business expanded, they never deviated from being an amusement company and was content with staying in the background. As far as Nintendo is concerned, in fact, McDonald's, Westin Hotels, Benesse and the Ministry of Education are all supporting Nintendo's game business from the bleachers, with Iwata smartly facilitating the trend.

He adheres firmly to a philosophy—call it "Amusement Fundamentalism," an unwritten code passed down through Nintendo's long history.

Protecting "Nintendo-ness"

Nintendo, having limited the scope of its business to this thing called "amusement," is an extremely compact organization. Iwata explains why.

"The things Nintendo does should be limited to the areas where we can display our greatest strengths. It's because we're good at throwing things away that we can fight these large battles using so few people. Yamauchi taught me that. If we couldn't pare things down, we'd never be able to compete with giant companies like Sony and Microsoft. We can't afford to diversify. Given that, we obviously have to team up with other companies to do the things we ourselves can't do, and the nature of those team-ups will keep on changing too, I think."

Nintendo focuses on its core competence—videogames—and borrows the expertise of other companies when it needs to. Even within the domain, Nintendo considers the manufacturing process of game consoles to be outside its purview.

Ever since the NES, Nintendo has entrusted the manufacture of its consoles to other companies—it is a so-called "fabless" company. They are thus able to focus on their strengths, devoting resources to pure hardware and software development.

Nintendo operations are exemplary when it comes to choosing and concentrating. The company has a strong tendency to avoid organizational bloat.

Progression of Nintendo Employee Total (Consolidated Basis)

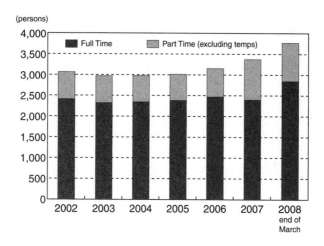

Given the success of the DS and the Wii, Nintendo has its hands full. Iwata explains.

"One of the things that makes Nintendo great, I think, is that right now we have overwhelmingly more ideas than we have people to implement them. When I meet one-on-one with Miyamoto, the same conversation happens over and over again: 'That's a great idea,' we'll agree, 'but we don't have enough people to do it.'"

Just as Iwata says, they can't turn more than a fraction of their ideas into software. So they need only hire more people, and there are thousands of applicants that would like to work for Nintendo, now that it's on top of the world. Yet the scale of the company's operations has changed very little.

Just before Iwata became president, around the end of March 2003, Nintendo's total workforce, including subsidiaries, was 3,073 people. Six years later, in March 2008, it had grown to 3,768.

During that span, the company's achievements had shot up, with sales roughly tripling, and net profits 2.4 times higher. Yet the growth in its workforce was only 1.23 times—relatively paltry. Excluding part-time and contract workers made the figure even lower—a growth

99

factor of only 1.17.

They could've grown by pursuing quick mergers and acquisitions. Fortunately, Nintendo has always held significant cash reserves, and is continuing its no-borrowing fiscal policy. In December 2008, its cash and cash-equivalent assets totaled more than one trillion yen.

But the only acquisition since the beginning of Iwata's tenure has been developer Monolith Soft, purchased from Bandai Namco Games in April 2007. While significant, the acquisition's figure was in the hundreds of millions of yen. Just before Nintendo's purchase, sales were 649 million yen—a small company.

From an investor's perspective, a cash reserve of one trillion yen is excessive, a useless asset that only serves to increase the denominator of the return on capital. Investment, after all, is the profession of taking a small amount of capital and turning a large profit with it. There are consequently investors who see Nintendo as having a poor efficiency of capital.

Choice and concentration is all fine and well. But since the amount of business they do has expanded far beyond the old days, and since they are so busy, many investors are pressing them to sink some money into growing their game operations.

But Nintendo has avoided using its cash reserves for large investments like M&A's and continues to pursue a policy of constantly saving money. Iwata's explanation of the reasoning: "The game platform business runs on momentum. When you fail, you can take serious damage. The risks are very high. And in that domain, Nintendo is making products that are totally unprecedented. Nobody can guarantee they won't fail. One big failure and boom—you're out two hundred, three hundred billion yen. In a business where a single flop can bankrupt you, you don't want to be set up like that."

And indeed, before Nintendo released the Wii, their production plans called for six million units to ship globally by March 2007, and to do that required securing component orders and production lines. 25,000 yen per unit times six million units equals 150 billion yen. Add the research and development costs to that, and the risk surpassed 200 billion yen.

"We're not aiming for the same things," Iwata says, "but if you go to the store, our console is competing with one from the richest, most successful company in the world, and one from the largest electronics maker in the world. To be completely honest, I don't think that even now we have enough [savings]."

Iwata furthermore explains another rationale behind the savings. For a fabless company that doesn't own manufacturing facilities, the cash is important as a guarantee of credit.

"All of Nintendo's hardware is built by outside partners. Even when we ask them to build something that goes off the roadmap, they trust we're not going to leave them holding the bag. That's why IBM, or NEC, or any number of other companies are willing to go along with us. We'd never be able to do what we do without being cash-rich."

Having maintained Nintendo's cash reserves, Iwata's response to investors was to increase the dividends paid to them. From 2005 it was raised to 50% or above, and in 2007, after years of dividends of 140 yen per share, they jumped to 1,260 yen. The payout ratio was at an extreme high of 63%. For 2008, dividends were expected to be even higher, reaching 1,370 yen.

Of course, it is not as though Iwata would never consider a major outlay. Assuming Nintendo's savings continue to accumulate, passing 1.5 trillion, perhaps even 2 trillion yen, a large merger or acquisition may become a possibility.

But there would be a condition, and it's that condition that gets to the very heart of why Nintendo is so wary of corporate expansion.

"If we decided to expand our workforce by ten times, we'd lose our Nintendo-ness."

Iwata uses this word, "Nintendo-ness," all the time. Nintendo is an unconventional company, and its corporate principles and culture are neither written nor explicitly articulated by anyone. Yet those who work for the company develop a common understanding of what

Nintendo-ness means.

It's something like the company's DNA, passed continuously along from person to person, ever since the Yamauchi era.

Once someone has grasped Nintendo-ness, it is rare for them to leave the company. That tendency protects and strengthens the company's lineage and makes employees feel at home. By the same token, a reckless merger would mean a flood of people who don't get Nintendo-ness and make the company less comfy.

"I often talk about this, but I'm still together with most of the members from 20 years ago. Sometimes someone has to quit because of family circumstances or what-have-you, but most of them are still around," says Miyamoto. He himself—as a world-famous game creator—has been the target of countless headhunting attempts, with serious salary offers. Yet he has always stayed with Nintendo, claiming "there's no place like this." Miyamoto is far from the only employee to be pursued by another company, yet nearly all of them decline.

While Nintendo's salaries are often said to be high, when compared with revenue per employee they can hardly be called excessive.

In September 2008, the British *Financial Times* gushed that Nintendo would earn a record $1.6 million per employee, a per-capita figure higher than Google ($626,000 per employee) and Goldman Sachs ($1.24 million per employee). But while Goldman Sachs's average salary was $660,000, the magazine reported, Nintendo's was only $99,000. The relatively low compensation for its employees was an important factor in boosting profit, *FT* concluded.

Something else, then, attracts talented people to Nintendo—and surely it is none other than the corporate DNA which yields Nintendo-ness. Adhering to and preserving that is the duty of those whose responsibility is the management of the company. Iwata explains: "If we became the kind of company that made anything, I think we would lose our individuality—we would lose what's good about us. We're strong because we're pointed, I think. That's what strength is about."

They avoid broadening their focus because they want to persist at what has always been their specialty: amusement. But amusement is a risky business, so Nintendo's bank accounts stay deep and their acquisitions few. The logic follows, but at its root is the ineffable will to preserve Nintendo-ness—which means not doing anything extraneous, not diversifying.

But what *is* Nintendo-ness? What is in the DNA of Nintendo? As something more felt than written, it is difficult to put into words. But when Iwata was pressed to explain what type of qualities he looked for when hiring, he offered a hint.

"Being original and flexible—in a sense, that's Nintendo's mission statement. It isn't written down anywhere, but ever since the Yamauchi era that's something Nintendo has always prized. Also, you have to love making people happy. To put it another way, you like to service. Yeah. Also you've got to have intellectual curiosity."

Growing up on Surprise and Delight

It was for the *Hobo Nikkan Itoi Shinbun* ("Almost-Daily Itoi News") blog that Iwata was talking about the days and nights in 1976 he spent endlessly programming on his first computer, back when he was a high school junior.

The man interviewing him was Shigesato Itoi—essayist, copywriter, and game designer for the famed SNES RPG *Earthbound*, released in 1994. Iwata—working at the time for Hal Laboratory—had lent a programming hand to the project, saving it from potential disaster.

The experience brought the two men together, and even after Iwata became president of Nintendo, he has stopped by Itoi's office a number of times.

> **Iwata:** Back in high school, there was this funny guy that sat next to me, and instead of listening to the math teacher or whoever's lecture, we'd play games.
> **Itoi:** Was this friend into computers too?
> **Iwata:** Yeah, he… how can I say it, he really loved the games I made—he was like my first customer. User Number One.
> **Itoi:** So it was like the class clown finding his audience.

[…]

Iwata: I feel like humans are a kind of creature that won't climb a tree unless they know somebody is going to be impressed or pleased with them. So meeting that guy back in high school had a huge influence on my life.

That high school scene became the bedrock experience for Iwata that set him down a path leading to the presidency of Nintendo. When asked if "making money" is the motivation that drives the company, this is how he answers.

"Making a splash. We want people to *like it*. That's why we do what we do, and the more people like our products, the greater our feeling of satisfaction. Our goal is always to make our customers glad—to have the things we make bring smiles to their faces."

Around the time when the Wii was released—the DS was already a hit—Iwata often spoke within Nintendo about the chain of smiles. Smiles because a game was fun, smiles because a game was getting parents and children to talk to each other, smiles because grandpa was hearty and hale no matter how old he was—Nintendo would do whatever it took to make their customers smile. A sense of meaning would make Nintendo's employees smile, too.

As a result their product would sell, retailers would smile, and so would investors thanks to improved performance. That chain of smiles is their ultimate mission, and so long as Nintendo can remain a corporation that can perpetuate it, they're satisfied that their responsibility to society is being fulfilled—that all the gears are properly meshed.

So what kind of company *is* Nintendo? Iwata smiles. "We're a manufacturer of smiles. I think that's what any entertainment company should be."

To make a splash, to put smiles on people's faces—in order to accomplish these missions, Nintendo requires two elements: surprise and delight.

Years ago, Nintendo introduced the Ray Gun, which used

photovoltaic cells as sensors, and with it, surprised and delighted the world. The Game & Watch series of handheld electronic games and the NES offered new-fangled machines and screens, and they brought delight to the people that played them. As semiconductor technology has matured, the pictures that videogames can display have gotten prettier. But in a world with high-definition displays and feature-packed cell phones, a fundamental fatigue with controlling images on a screen brought about a decline in the game business.

Yet the beleaguered Nintendo endured, finally introducing, once again, new-fangled game systems with new-fangled games. They surprised the world, and therein lay their success. But, easier said than done. Can Nintendo bear the pain and burden of having to deliver surprises over and over again?

"When our customers are surprised, or happy, we're receiving the best reward there is, and it gives us energy. Even someone as talented as Miyamoto would have trouble working if you cut him off from all feedback. It's fun for us when we see people's reactions, and it's what lets us keep doing our job," says Iwata, summarily dismissing any anxiety about pain or burden. What, then, of Miyamoto, whose prowess is always being tested as a game creator followed by the entire world? Let's lean on him for some answers.

—Don't you get tired of always trying to surprise people?
No way.
—Do you ever get to the place where you think, that's it, I'm all out of ideas?
I say that every year. (laugh)
—Can you see where the next surprise is going to come from?
Not at all. I've gotten by all these years without being able to see that. Every time I look back after five years, though, I realize I had no idea where I'd end up, so y'know, things work out. I don't worry about not being able to do it.
—You don't feel pressure?
Feeling pressure, that wears you out. I just try to think about how to have as much fun as I can doing my job.

Progression of Nintendo's R&D Budget

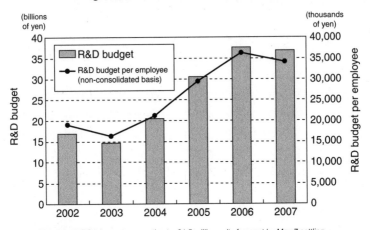

Note: Global total. DS 5th quarter an estimate, 31.5 million units forecast by May 7 settling.
Source: Nintendo

Nintendo is run by people who feed on surprise and delight, and the company feeds on the results. Of course, without the right conditions in place, no surprises are possible. But Nintendo has created that environment—with an abundance of "funds," without which surprises cannot be.

As discussed previously, Nintendo's individual compensation is not extraordinarily high. Miyamoto has been offered higher salaries from competitors in an effort to lure him away. But he has stayed, since at Nintendo he commands a budget that dwarfs any salary offer, a budget for the creation of surprise and delight. In his own words:

"Money they pay you and money you get to use for work are totally different things. I realized that very early on. For our main developers, there's actually no budget (laugh). No, don't worry, we're very careful about managing it. But we have it good, the company tells us we can use what money we need."

And Nintendo's R&D budget is always increasing. In 2007 it was 37 billion yen. If you posit that every employee has authority over its disposal, that works out to a staggering 35 million yen per employee.

By the same calculation, Canon comes out to 12 million, about a third of Nintendo's budget.

Moreover, the company does not put a lot of pressure on the people pursuing that research. Iwata explains that Nintendo is not a company where extensive meetings, presentations, negotiations, and oversight are required to push through a proposal.

"For example, if Miyamoto had to spend half his time and energy figuring out how to get the budget he needed, I don't think he'd have nearly the creative power he has at his age. He understood the value of that situation early in his career."

Incidentally, on November 16, 2008, Miyamoto celebrated his 56th birthday. Perhaps he's turned that surprise and delight into vitality, because he's visibly shot through with a youthful spirit that makes it impossible to imagine he's just four years away from the age of retirement.

Nintendo, likewise, takes the surprise and delight it brings the world and turns it into corporate vitality. In that sense, it overlaps with a certain computer company from Cupertino, California.

Apple and Nintendo—Less Alike Than They Appear

In Tokyo's exclusive Ginza district, across the street from the storied Matsuya department store, is Apple's flagship Tokyo store. This correspondent visited the location one day in November 2008.

Waiting on the fourth floor was Phil Schiller, vice president of worldwide product marketing for Apple. He is considered the firm's No. 2 man along with Tim Cook, chief operating officer and Steve Jobs's right hand.

Holding a new laptop that had just been released, he feverishly explained how revolutionary and unique it was. PR wanted to limit questions to those pertaining to the new product, but there was one that just had to be asked. Some people had the impression that Apple and Nintendo were similar. What did he think? Phil Schiller was graceful enough to take that one.

"I think they have a lot in common with us in that we both make unique, interesting products that surprise people. I really respect and think highly of Nintendo. I myself own a Gamecube and a Wii."

Straight from the horse's mouth.

In 2008, the progressive commoditization of the personal computer market brought prices down to a new low. Computer makers put out $500 "netbooks" that were good for web browsing and email. Prices continued to fall, and by the end of 2008, $300 machines were out.

Amid this trend, in October 2008, Apple unveiled their redesigned notebook computer, the MacBook, a premium machine that defied the low-price trend.

"The unibody, machined from a single slab of aluminum, is a huge breakthrough," said Schiller. "Aluminum is light and durable, and looks good too. It opened up a new era for our notebooks."

Just as Schiller said, the beautiful, seamless chassis was a sight to behold. Its unique, laser-machined design clearly distinguished it from other companies' notebook offerings.

The best part was the glass multitouch trackpad. Touching it with a single finger let you move the cursor as in a standard trackpad, but using two fingers let you scroll window contents horizontally and vertically. By pinching and spreading two fingers, you could zoom in and out of images, just like on Apple's iPhone, and swiping left or right with three fingers let you move back and forth through pictures in an album.

All of these ideas were protected by patents, making them difficult for other companies to copy. At the same time, Apple seemed to have no interest in the low-cost PC market that other companies were scrambling to get into. When asked about it, this was Schiller's answer: "The Macbook has a lot of features that people didn't realize they wanted until they're offered. There may be a lot of people out there willing to forego features for a lower price, but we're ahead of other companies in bringing out new value. That's how we've led the market. That priority won't change."

Undaunted by Microsoft, whose OS has a 90% share of the market, Apple continues to wow consumers with its innovative products. While other companies race to the bottom of cheap, low-end computers, Apple did fine globally with its new MacBook, which started at 148,800 yen.

In the last quarter of 2008, Apple's computer sales were up 9%. Its notebook sales were up 34%, thank to the redesigned MacBook. According to market intelligence firm IDC, worldwide computer sales actually *declined* 0.4% during that quarter. Apple had achieved growth in poor market conditions.

The iPod. The iPhone. Apple doesn't make ordinary products. They concentrate on delivering fun, surprising products, and consumers are willing to pay for that value. Apple takes pride in its software development, bringing new experiences to its customers on the twin pillars of hardware and software.

On that count, it's certainly not unlike Nintendo. Iwata himself agrees:

"We want people to be surprised, and we want people to call our approach unique. That's what people say about Apple, too. So I think, yeah, we may be making different things, but pursue a certain focus and you get a lot of commonalities."

It's not just the business methodology of the two companies that seems similar. Their performance charts are practically congruent upward-trending lines.

Interestingly, like Nintendo, Apple also weathered a difficult period, during which sales of its Mac computers were poor. Its recovery began in 2000, when Steve Jobs returned to the company after a long absence—coincidentally, the same year Iwata came to Nintendo.

Design, software, surprise, fun... Jobs brought the keywords that exemplified "Apple-ness" back to the forefront, which gave rise to the iPod and turned the company's fortunes around. Building on the iPod's success, Jobs began a counterattack on the personal computer front as well. Just as the DS was followed by the Wii.

Both Apple and Nintendo freed themselves from slumps and went on to enjoy incredible comebacks. Both have come to enjoy high expectations from consumers, investors, and pundits alike, all of

Apple and Nintendo: Business Performance

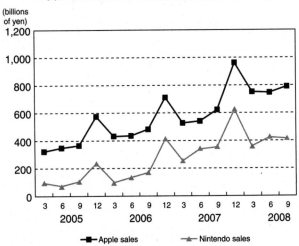

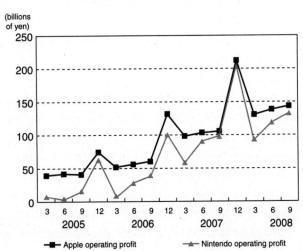

whom wait for each company's announcement with bated breath.

Miyamoto expresses the progress of the two companies this way. "I think there are a lot of things we have in common—I think both companies are extremely good at predicting how their customers will react. I guess I shouldn't say that about my own company, though. But yes, I think we're quite conscious of such things, and both [Nintendo and Apple] do their business with an acute sense of what will go over well."

Incidentally, Iwata is an Apple fan of 20 years. He's had his beloved MacBook for ages and uses the same presentation software that Steve Jobs uses—Keynote—to prepare his balance sheet materials. He's used an iPod since the very first model and has purchased every new iteration to the bemusement of those around him. And of course, he has an iPhone.

Yet Iwata doesn't forget to emphasize one difference between the two companies.

"We've done all sorts of things to play to our strengths, to paint a bright future for ourselves, and in the end people have started to say, 'Wow, Nintendo's a lot like Apple.' But we're an amusement company, and Apple's a tech company. There are lots of differences that arise from that."

Amusement and technology—put another way, one makes toys, and the other makes appliances. It's hard to get along these days without a computer. Likewise a cell phone. And though a portable music player may technically be for amusement, many people consider them indispensable.

But you don't need a videogame console to live. It's not the kind of thing that's meant to make your daily life more convenient. With PCs able to play videogames at home, and iPods and cell phones doubling as game machines on the go, dedicated game systems are becoming less necessary every year.

It is this circumstance that Nintendo has been confronting and fighting.

It is for this reason—and with pride—that Iwata ultimately

concludes that "there are lots of differences."

Strength From Useless Things

In order to be as familiar and unintimidating as possible, the Wii Remote was inspired by a simple television remote control. But in March 2008, Nintendo took that to the next level—it became an *actual* TV remote.

"The program guides on modern digital TVs are pretty good. But when I want to find a show, scrolling through a week's worth of listings to get to it feels like it takes all day—it's just so unresponsive. So I thought about trying to make a guide that could switch screens really quickly."

Iwata's idea became the Television Friend Channel, a new channel for the Wii. It's free, and can be used on any TV, for both digital and analog broadcast or cable programming. It displays eight days' worth of programming schedules, in three dimensions. Clicking on a day or time slot zooms in to show more detailed information.

The controls are simplicity itself.

A digital TV's built-in guide hardly compares. The responsiveness of the Television Friend Channel far outstrips that of a DVR, allowing effortless browsing and searching of listings. Selecting a performer's name from an individual listing instantly shows other shows in which they appear, all in three dimensions.

Users can stamp their favorite shows and have text messages sent to themselves or their friends when its air time is approaching. Favorite stamps of users nationwide are collected, and users can easily discover what shows are popular, and with what demographic.

Clicking on a program name or channel switches to the relevant broadcast. The Wii Remote's directional pad controls the TV's volume and channel, and when the user's finished watching, pushing the home button brings them back to the Wii menu.

In other words, the Wii could now function as the gateway to both videogames and television broadcasts.

The impact of the Television Friend Channel was bigger on the television and electronics industries than it was for Wii users—the Wii had taken over as the user interface for the television.

The TV, after all, was the territory of electronics companies and broadcasters. Videogames merely borrowed the screen for a while. But if a game system could now motivate channel selection, then the master-servant situation had suddenly been reversed.

What was worse, the built-in user interfaces for televisions were an important arena of differentiation for electronics makers. They had pursued user-friendly displays and functional grace over decades of research. It represented a significant source of pride.

But the ease of use that the outsider Wii now offered was great enough to completely destroy that pride. "Game companies live and die by their products' reaction speed and ease of use. If your customers are annoyed, you lose. If they don't get it, you lose. We realized that was a relative strength of ours, and applied to the TV program screen, that's what we got," explains Iwata of the project.

There are other channels on the Wii Menu that exemplify this strength.

For example, the Wii Photo Channel takes your series of memorable photographs and turns it into a beautiful slideshow, complete with a nostalgic piano tune playing in the background. Panning upward, zooming out, the Photo Channel's slideshow function stages an experience reminiscent of the end roll of a documentary.

To Iwata's way of thinking, amusement companies are subject to an intense pressure that appliance companies never feel. "For a long time," he explains, "we've made things that are fundamentally useless. People won't endure inconvenience that they don't have to endure. They won't read your instruction manual. If something is hard to understand, it's entirely the maker's fault. If they can't figure out a videogame in five minutes, then in their mind it's a 'crappy game' and that's the end of it."

Appliances, on the other hand, could count on people needing to use them, forcing users to read the instruction manual. If it's a bit difficult to use, they put up with it. But that kind of complacency won't fly in a videogame. People won't overlook irritating elements

113

while they're at play—and so Nintendo has accrued over 20 years of experience of trying to make things fun and easy.

In their efforts to bring gaming to the mainstream, Nintendo has gone past traditional videogames and stepped into a larger domain. In doing so, they realized the gap that existed between them and other companies when it came to packaging "ease"—and they realized the potential that lay therein.

"Even when they're playing so-called 'practical' games for the DS or Wii, people can use them easily and intuitively without having to read the manual, and it makes them smile. That's the know-how we've built up over 20 years," says Iwata.

He first put that know-how to use on games like *Brain Age* and *English Training*. Once those games had proven their success on the DS, Wii software was next—the games that help players improve their fitness are good examples. Then, transcending games entirely, came software that turned the DS into an information terminal and the Wii into a photo gallery, both of which thoroughly demonstrate the strength that comes from being an amusement company.

Even Miyamoto, the inveterate game creator, has realized the potential he has in other arenas. "A Wii-connected television is way easier to use than a regular TV. It makes me wish they'd let us just handle the whole thing (laugh). Electronics companies have really dropped the ball when it comes to the interfaces to their products. But that's where we think hardest, and we've been competing in the toughest of environments."

Nintendo's talent at ease has been honed through fierce competition in the amusement market, and it's an important weapon. But that same fierce competition has given them another weapon, too.

A Charred Game Boy

Nintendo has a retail store, "Nintendo World," in New York City's Rockefeller Center. In it is displayed a legendary Game Boy unit.

The charred, blacked system is housed in a glass display case. On the screen runs a *Tetris* demo. On the lower left side of the case is an explanatory plaque—"Game Boy damaged in Gulf War." It survived an aerial bombing in the first Gulf War.

Sooty and burned, warped by the heat of the blast, the damaged Game Boy was recovered and donated to Nintendo World. As the note on the plaque reads, "It still works!"

Elsewhere, the highest point on the globe—Mt. Everest. After he reached the peak on June 2, 2005, Neil Mueller delivered the following report to news media: "I brought a DS, a notebook computer, and an MP3 player to Everest, but only the DS was tough enough to hang in there until the very end. The others gave into the wind and cold, and broke."

There are countless other "legends of hardiness" about Nintendo's products around the world. Half of them seem to involve normal use, while the other half are deliberate tests of durability—many of which have been uploaded to video-sharing sites like YouTube, becoming quite popular on the net as they circulate.

One video has a PS2, an Xbox, and a GameCube—an iron ball is dropped on each one, then they are hit with a hammer and dropped from the second floor onto the ground. The last cut shows the GameCube to be the only machine that still functions after all that. Another has a GameCube being dragged around on rope behind a moving car—and it still works.

Nintendo workers would have a hard time watching the ridiculous scenes. The consoles were never made with such treatment in mind, so the videos are hardly useful as reference. Yet they are very effective demonstrations of the robustness of Nintendo's hardware.

"I think our quality standards are quite a bit higher than most electronics companies," says Miyamoto, and it's true. Nintendo's durability criteria are quite stringent. They did not sacrifice toughness for compactness even when designing the DS and Wii.

In the case of their portable console, it did not go into production until it could pass a difficult test. It had to work consistently after being dropped ten times from a height of 1.5 meters, higher than an adult's breast pocket.

Iwata explains. "If a kid puts a game console in the basket of their bicycle, then has to make a sudden stop, the console can come flying

U.S. troops playing Nintendo games at a base in northern Kuwait in March 2003, at the time of the war in Iraq. [Photo © Getty Images]

out—and it's not going to land on carpet. So I told them to make it so it could survive being dropped from 1.5 meters onto concrete. The hardware design team screamed, but proceeded to figure out how to pass the test."

In the case of the DS, they dropped dozens of prototypes 100 times each, measuring how many drops it took to break each one, then choosing the most durable design. With the Wii—which would normally be stationary—the design had to be able to withstand an 80 kg weight for one minute.

Normally, if someone drops an electronic device and breaks it, the fault is their own. Nintendo, however, is obsessed about the durability of their systems due to an overriding fear that a customer who gets upset over a broken system might never give them another chance.

Which is why Nintendo's customer support is courteous to the point of excess.

The Wii was released in the US in November 2006, just before its Japanese release. Almost immediately, video of people playing the new system began appearing on YouTube, and Wii mishaps were among the most popular.

In one, a young man is playing the tennis game in *Wii Sport*. The Wii Remote only needs gentle movements to operate, but the young man flails around with all his strength—at which point the strap that secures the Wii Remote to the player's wrist breaks, and the Wii Remote goes flying into the wall.

Videos of accidentally thrown Wii Remotes breaking light bulbs and glass windows and cracking TV screens began to circulate. Given that they were filmed, not all of them could have been genuine accidents. Some players simply ignored the on-screen exhortation to secure the wrist strap, while others looked like they were deliberately throwing the remote.

Nevertheless, Nintendo's response was quick.

In December 2006, less than a month after the Wii's release in the US, Nintendo offered new, strengthened straps free of charge to anyone who had purchased the console at the time of the first shipment.

117

Consoles sold after that point came with the newly designed strap. Worldwide, 3.2 million Wii Remotes benefited from the offer.

Moreover, in October 2007, Nintendo issued the following announcement: "At Nintendo we are constantly working to improve the safety of our products. We'd like to announce at this time that as part of those efforts, we've developed a protective cover for the Wii Remote—which we're calling the Wii Remote Jacket—which will be offered free of charge to all Wii owners."

The Wii Jacket would be included with all new Wii systems shipping after that date, but like the strap, it was to be given away free of charge to anyone who had already bought a Wii—Nintendo would even pay the postage. Over 15 million units had to be delivered. Iwata, who made the decision, explains it. "If I may say so myself, without a corporate culture like ours, you just wouldn't do that. But we work in order to make our customers smile, and if even one out of ten million of them isn't happy, we don't like that."

Development on the Wii Remote Jacket started after looking at customer's reactions to the remote itself. Unlike the strap, the jacket covers the entire remote, which can affect its control characteristics. And like before, they created dozens of prototypes in order to find the optimum material and shape, one that would cushion the remote if it were accidentally thrown or hit someone, yet would preserve usability.

Iwata explains the company's decision to shoulder the costs of both developing the jacket and giving it away for free as though it were the most obvious thing in the world. "It was a no-brainer. Or rather, when we discussed the matter within the company, not one person suggested that it would cost too much and therefore shouldn't be done."

Of course, given the issue's notoriety on YouTube, from a certain perspective, Nintendo couldn't afford *not* to act. But Nintendo has long been a company that provides support that borders on the excessive even when it's not visible. That's just the kind of company they are.

There is another story, of a man in the city of Takarazuka, in Japan's Hyogo prefecture. When he took his DS out of his backpack one day, he noticed that the plastic cover of the left end of the hinge between the upper and lower screens was cracking. It was still within warranty, so he contacted Nintendo's customer support, and was told, "Send it to us, at our expense."

The initial estimate for repair time was two weeks. The repair facility said that the touch panel was also malfunctioning. The man waited, impressed. "Considering the cost, I would have assumed it would have been cheaper to just replace it, but they were repairing it."

But then, a week later, a new DS arrived—but that wasn't what surprised the man. He had applied a sticker to the upper part of his old DS, and that same sticker had been carefully stuck on the same place of this new DS.

The Nintendo support center had tried to repair the original unit, but had then determined that it would be better to simply replace it—and had then carefully peeled the sticker off the old unit and applied it to the new. On top of that, they had also carefully removed a protective film the man had been using on the touch screen of his old DS, and sent it back to him in a clear plastic bag.

Nintendo is originally a toy company. Children are attached to their toys, and repairs are not necessarily so simple as sending a brand-new replacement. The man saw this transaction not as a simple repair, but rather as a "message" that Nintendo took its role as a toy company very seriously.

This sticker episode is far from unique. The blogosphere is full of reports of new units coming back with old stickers carefully reapplied to them—the touching stories are a hot topic on the internet.

Users around the globe are coming to share the common view that Nintendo products don't break—and even if they do, it'll be okay.

But Nintendo did not earn that reputation by actively trying to get it.

They simply understood that because they were an amusement

company that made useless things instead of useful appliances, negative or problematic elements had to be removed from their products, or they would have no future at all. Their reputation was nothing other than the result of constant efforts to be correct with their customers.

Put another way, Nintendo's strength and reputation comes from its tireless experience of making "useless things" and from its sincere acceptance of the fate of an amusement company: if customers somehow fail to have fun, they'll easily turn away.

That's the way it's been ever since Gunpei Yokoi developed the Game Boy, and the Game & Watch series.

5

Game & Watch:
The Toy That Started It All

"At its heart, making toys is about using existing technology skillfully to deliver a surprising experience. It's not a matter of whether or not the tech is cutting edge, but whether or not people think it's fun."

—Iwata

The Revival of Lateral Thinking

In a room, a child fires a toy gun. A laser-like beam issues from the barrel, reflecting off a mirror to hit a target set in the forehead of a plastic lion. The lion gives a great roar, its eyes flashing.

This TV commercial set aflame the heart and desire of many a child. It advertised a 1970 toy from Nintendo, the "Kousenjuu SP" ("Ray Gun SP").

It sold for 4,780 yen. At the time, that made it a rather expensive toy, but it nonetheless became a calling-card hit for Nintendo and a regular fixture as a Christmas or birthday gift.

The man responsible for this product was Gunpei Yokoi, the first head of Nintendo's development section (later known as Development Section One), which handled all new toys at Nintendo.

Some thirty-odd years later, the same company would release the DS and Wii. Iwata lumps these two products in with the ray gun.

"I think the old products that are the most similar are the ones that Yokoi worked on. For example, take the ray gun—it didn't use cutting-edge technology. But the idea of using a photovoltaic cell as a sensor, that was incredible. It was perfect for using as a sensor instead of a power source. It's representative of the kind of thing that's part of Nintendo's DNA, I feel."

The ray gun didn't shoot bullets, nor did it fire a beam the way it seemed to in the commercial. Yet the target would only react when the gun was accurately aimed. For children who were used to the cheap rubber pellet guns they could get at the drugstore, the ray gun was a high-tech, electronic revelation.

But its construction was simplicity itself.

Hidden in the barrel of the rifle was a small light bulb, and when the trigger was pulled, a spring-loaded shutter would click open. A sensor installed in the target would detect the flicker of light and trip the target's hit mechanism.

The bulb was slightly recessed in the gun's barrel, so unless it was pointed directly at the target, the light wouldn't reach the sensor, and no hit would be registered. For the sensor, Yokoi used a photovoltaic cell—the same technology used in solar panels. This was the key to the ray gun.

Normally photovoltaic cells are used to generate electricity. But when Yokoi noticed that the photovoltaics a Sharp sales rep had brought him were sensitive to even slight changes in light, he had the novel notion that the cell could be used as a target sensor, and quickly put it to use in a toy.

From only a light bulb and a photovoltaic cell came an unheard-of new kind of play—exactly the kind of surprise and delight Nintendo strives for. It amply demonstrated Yokoi's true worth—as did 1980's Game & Watch series.

In the 1970s, electronics makers fought the "Calculator Wars," which spread from office products to the home market to a one-calculator-per-person level. The fight was sparked by Casio in 1972 when they unveiled their "Casio Mini."

The Casio Mini sent a shockwave through every company that had a stake in the calculator market. It was a quarter the size of other calculators at the time, and its price had been kept low—at 12,800 yen, it was about a third as expensive as its competitors. It was an explosive hit, breaking the million-unit barrier within ten months of its introduction and eventually going on to sell ten million units. It recast the terms of the conflict in the direction of lower prices and miniaturization.

Many of its competitors withdrew from the marketplace thereafter, leaving Casio to compete with the likes of Sharp. In 1983, Casio introduced a solar-powered calculator that was only 0.8 millimeters thick, which effectively ended the war.

During this time, manufacturing costs fell dramatically. Technology matured—LSI (Large-Scale Integration) made calculator circuits smaller, and readability improved with the introduction of segmented

Using quite simple technology, Yokoi staged surprises and delights no one had imagined. Yokoi's philosophy gave birth to hit products like the Ray Gun and the Game & Watch and contributed to the Wii Remote. [Photo © Tetsuya Yamada]

numeric liquid crystal readouts.

It was this mature technology that Yokoi would put to use for the Game & Watch series.

The moment that led to Game & Watch's creation came on a business trip. Yokoi was riding the bullet train, and he noticed a salaryman on the train fiddling with his calculator to while the time away.

He wondered: would it be possible to create a game the size of a calculator, that could fit unobtrusively in a commuter's hand and be an easy way to kill some time? Yokoi mentioned his flash of insight to then-president Yamauchi when the two men happened to be riding in the same car, and the conversation proceeded from there.

The series saw the light of day in 1980, with its first game, *Ball*. The object of the simple game—which was easily held, and used only two buttons—was to move two "hands" displayed on the screen in order to juggle multiple balls. It sold for 5,800 yen, roughly as much as a pocket calculator at the time, and was instantly successful.

Unlike the DS, the Game & Watch series was not cartridge-based; each model played a single game. Not one to let the opportunity escape him, Yokoi produced a variety of different games, which also sold well. Over a span of eight years, beginning in 1980, 70 Game & Watch variants were sold, with the total number of units sold passing 48 million.

This massive success was an excellent illustration of Yokoi's famous dictum: "Lateral thinking with seasoned technology." Game & Watch had come from taking the parts and mature technology that had gone into pocket calculators and applying them to an amusement product with a completely different goal and use.

The philosophy went all the way back to the delightful ray gun and its use of seasoned technologies like light bulbs and photovoltaic cells—where a light bulb was used not as a light source, but as a bullet, and a photovoltaic cell was used not to generate power, but to sense that bullet.

It was thanks to unexpected applications of mature technology that Nintendo was able to offer novel, fun toys at prices that made them plausible as gifts for children. It is a philosophy that was close to Yokoi's heart, and it has been passed on to the new Nintendo.

The Wii's defining characteristic is its novel controller, the Wii Remote, whose conception and execution could only have come from Nintendo.

The top of the remote houses a CMOS image sensor, not unlike the kind found in digital cameras or cell phones. Opposite it, in the left and right ends of the "sensor bar" placed either above or below the television, are infrared LEDs of the sort commonly used in conventional remote controls. Both components are old news, easily available in any Akihabara electronics store. Since they're both manufactured and sold in huge quantities around the globe, they're cheap—the LEDs cost but only a few dozen yen each.

The principle behind the controller's pointer functionality is simple. The CMOS image sensor housed in the Wii Remote senses the position of the two infrared light sources in the sensor bar. It wirelessly sends that positional information to the Wii console. Based on that information, the console computes where on the TV screen the Wii Remote is pointing, and updates the image on the screen accordingly.

In fact, so long as there are two sources of infrared light near the television, the Wii Remote will function correctly, whether or not that source is the sensor bar. In reality, you can make your own sensor bar for a few hundred yen worth of parts, and on the internet, fans have even shared videos of people playing with two candles set up in front of the TV.

In other words, the Wii Remote employs a camera component intended for taking pictures as a sensor to track position, and a component intended for transmitting signals as a simple marker—a perfect example of lateral thinking.

Yokoi's philosophy is also evident in the previously mentioned use of the Wii Remote as a television control.

When using the Wii Menu's Television Friend Channel, the Wii

Remote can control the TV channel and volume.

A normal television remote has an infrared LED at its end, which sends signals to the TV in order to control it. But the Wii Remote has no such LEDs.

The Wii console's video output is analog, and the cable transmits only the video and audio signals. It does not use the recent HDMI standard that would allow it to control other devices. So how does the Wii Remote control the TV?

The answer is the infrared LEDs in the sensor bar.

Only when the user initiates a channel change on the TV, the sensor bar sends an appropriate infrared signal, which reflects off the opposite wall and hits the TV's remote sensor. Thanks to lateral thinking, the sensor bar—normally used only to determine the orientation of the Wii Remote—becomes part of an actual remote control. It's almost like cheating.

Yokoi's strategy of lateral thinking with seasoned technology is still relevant to Nintendo today.

"At its heart, making toys is about using existing technology skillfully to deliver a surprising experience. It's not a matter of whether or not the tech is cutting edge, but whether or not people think it's fun," says Iwata, who took Yokoi's thinking to heart not only with the minute details of the Wii's construction, but with the design philosophy of the platform as a whole.

The Wii gave up trying to compete on ultra-high resolution graphics, and chose instead to use hardware roughly on par with the previous generation. Whereas the rival PS3 and Xbox 360 systems generate HD images, the Wii outputs DVD-level SD graphics equivalent to the GameCube and PS2 systems that came before it.

But by deemphasizing the graphics and CPU of the system, the Wii's costs were kept down, and the developers were free to focus on things like a new, intuitive controller and built-in connectivity functions, drawing a clear distinction between itself and its competition.

And in the end, two years after its release, the Wii is the clear victor.

The same can be said of the DS. Its screen resolution is a mere 256x192, lower even than the 1seg standard for cell phone video broadcasting in Japan. By contrast, the rival PSP boasts resolution of 480x272, 2.7 times as many pixels as the DS. Instead—in another example of lateral thinking—the DS delivers fun to its users via a well-worn piece of technology from PDAs: a touch screen.

Using bleeding-edge technology to produce brilliant graphics and music does not guarantee people will have fun, but taking a new look at old technology can give rise to surprisingly delightful toys.

The DS and Wii are the result of Nintendo harkening back to a philosophy that could reasonably be called its origin.

Yokoi was the man who left Nintendo that legacy, and his influence on the company is impossible to overstate.

Gunpei Yokoi, The Genius of Play

The United States had commenced bombing North Vietnam, and with US-Soviet tensions running high, the entire world was being sucked into the gloom of the Cold War. It was 1965, and a certain optimistic young man had just graduated college and gone to work for Nintendo. His name was Gunpei Yokoi, and he was 23 years old.

When Yokoi joined, the company had just transitioned from being Nintendo of the traditional *hanafuda* cards to Nintendo of the Western-style playing cards. They had introduced the first plastic playing cards to Japan in 1953, to great success. In 1959, Nintendo negotiated with Disney to release Disney-themed cards, which were likewise an unprecedented hit.

After being so successful with their playing cards, in 1962 Nintendo went public on the Osaka Securities Exchange. With the money raised from their stock listing, they began to grope their way toward diversification of their operations, but their efforts had yet to mature.

Yokoi had hoped to go to work for a major electronics maker, where he could put the electrical engineering degree he'd earned at Doshisha University to use—but he was turned away at every one.

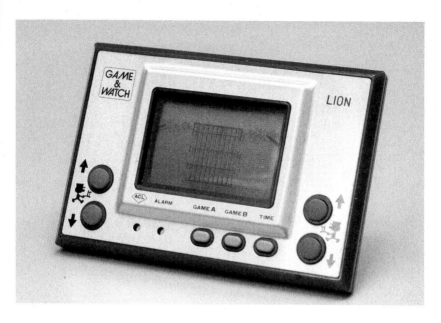

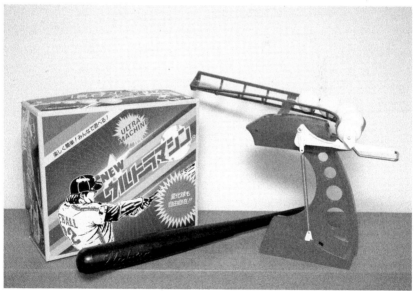

A salaryman playing with his calculator on a bullet train to kill time inspired the Game & Watch (above), a hit product with a total of 48 million units sold. Pictured below it is the Ultra Machine. [Photo © Tetsuya Yamada]

Though Nintendo had yet to so much as write the first letter of the word "electronic," Yokoi applied to the company—they were located in his hometown—and as luck would have it, they were the only company that would have him. He was the first person with a technology background they had ever hired.

At the time, he had no way of knowing he would alter Nintendo's course forever.

As he had an electrical engineering degree, Yokoi was assigned to do maintenance inspections on the card-manufacturing equipment. It left him with significant free time, but since he was the kind of person who had no trouble amusing himself, he passed the days without any particular resentment.

One day Yokoi was fiddling around with a toy he'd made with the factory's lathe; it was a series of interlocking lattices that could expand and contract. President Yamauchi saw this and called Yokoi into his office. Yokoi was worried he was in for some serious scolding.

"Nintendo is a game maker," Yamauchi said, "so turn that thing into a game and sell it."

Thus in 1966, just a year after Yokoi joined Nintendo, was born the Ultra Hand, an extending gripper-arm that could grab distant objects and bring them to the user.

Yokoi was a self-proclaimed "academic failure," but the product of his whim and the president's ultimatum was a toy that sold one million units. As a result, Yokoi was taken off maintenance duty and given charge of Nintendo's first "research and development section," where he would work hard to create new toy concepts.

The first product to come out of the section was the Ultra Machine, an indoor batting practice game. It was a hit. The next year, 1969, saw the release of the singular Love Tester.

The Love Tester claimed to measure the degree of affection between a man and a woman. Couples wishing to be so measured would hold hands, then each grab hold of an electrode with their free hand. The toy's meter would then register their putative compatibility.

In the only written account he left behind, a book entitled *Yokoi*

Gunpei Game Kan ("Gunpei Yokoi's Game House") Yokoi confessed as follows:

> I'd majored in electrical engineering. If I didn't do something electronic I'd look bad, but then anything too complicated was out of the question. I was just playing around with resistance measurements on a multimeter when I noticed there was some electrical current running through the human body. The Love Tester came from me wondering if I could somehow use this to get girls to hold my hand. [...] I wound up holding hands with quite a few girls thanks to it. Of course, somewhere along the line I started to feel like I wanted to do more than just hold hands. (laugh)

Yokoi had a reputation as something of a playboy—he'd done ballroom dance in college, played music, drove around in foreign cars, and spent his summers diving—so this confession was very much in character.

If it wasn't fun, it couldn't be a toy. The Love Tester condensed Yokoi's playful spirit into a physical product, and at the same time, it was an electronic toy that established the ultimately epochal philosophy of lateral thinking with seasoned technology.

The Love Tester merely measured electrical current running through an object. Even at the time, the components to build it could be had at any hardware store—surely the very definition of mature technology.

Lateral thinking turned this simple tool into a machine that tested the love between a man and woman—purportedly.

And yet it was not an entirely baseless gag toy. According to Yokoi's theory, couples with stronger feelings would be more likely to be nervous around each other, causing their hands to sweat, which would lower electrical resistance. If they were to kiss while using the device, current would also pass through their saliva, causing the meter to jump still higher.

The Love Tester was the impetus for Yokoi to devote himself to electronic toy creation, which in turn led to the previously mentioned

Ray Gun and Game & Watch, both of which would become signature Nintendo products.

It is worth saying that the NES, which turned Nintendo into a worldwide household name, was not a Yokoi product. It was developed by Masayuki Uemura, who had transferred to Nintendo from Sharp.

In 1979, President Yamauchi gave a new research and development section—R&D 2—to Uemura, and around the autumn of 1982, development of the NES began. At the time, Yokoi was feverishly working on the follow-up to Game & Watch.

But without the foundation for electronic toys that Yokoi had laid with Game & Watch, the NES would never have been developed, and without the funds that came from Game & Watch's success, Nintendo wouldn't have been able to afford its development. In that sense, Yokoi's contribution to the NES was a large one.

He also made an important contribution of human resources.

The game that touched off the NES's explosive success was *Super Mario Bros.*, which featured Miyamoto's character design. The one who brought Miyamoto into R&D after four years at Nintendo and gave him the chance to create games was none other than Yokoi.

Miyamoto's debut as a game creator was *Donkey Kong*, a commercial arcade machine and the ultimate form of a game Yokoi had been working on as another entry in the Game & Watch series: *Popeye*.

Yokoi asked Miyamoto if he would be interested in developing *Popeye* together for Game & Watch, and the idea was soon shifted to arcade use. However, as previously discussed, copyright issues prevented use of the Popeye intellectual property.

"Hey, Miyamoto, why don't you come up with some new character?" said Yokoi, and thus was born the indomitable Mario and his rival, Donkey Kong.

Donkey Kong was released to huge success in the US, and in 1982 it was ported and released on a new dual-screened Game & Watch unit. It was Yokoi's biggest hit in the series, and in order to make both horizontal and vertical control accessible, he equipped the system with a directional pad—the world's first.

The directional pad would also later contribute to the NES's success.

Existing game controllers were limited to round or square buttons or a "joystick" for directional control. After much trial and error in obtaining joystick-like control for Game & Watch, he eventually arrived at the thin, durable directional pad.

It goes without saying that this was the origin of the directional pad used on the NES controller. The lever on the NES console that ejected the game cartridge was also based on an idea of Yokoi's; he had a significant influence on the hardware aspect of the project as well.

It's not an overstatement to say that without Yokoi, the NES wouldn't have succeeded.

And his influence did not end there. After Sony took control of the home console market, Nintendo was supported through those dark times by its portable consoles.

The Game Boy: Low-Tech Victory

After the explosive success of the Game & Watch series, the R&D 1 group that Yokoi led seemed to lose its energy in direct proportion to R&D 2's gains, as the latter turned the NES into a hit.

The NES was introduced in 1983, and with its popular series of games that included the *Super Mario Bros.* series, created and conquered the modern home videogame market. Its business model had outside software developers writing games for the NES, which Nintendo would then distribute, taking a commission from each sale. It was massively profitable.

Meanwhile, the popularity of the Game & Watch series had begun to abate, and R&D 1 had finished the bulk of development work on a sequel series. The department now started on innovative projects for the NES, including a light-gun game called *Wild Gunman* (which took its inspiration from Yokoi's ray gun) and a robotic peripheral called *R.O.B.*, which could read commands from the TV screen and physically pick up blocks or game pieces as directed.

But none of these led to hits, and R&D 1's once-mighty presence within the company was waning.

Nonetheless, Yokoi did not cease development. The great task that was a multi-game Game & Watch system still lay ahead. It would be a portable system, yet would feature NES-like interchangeable cartridges. It was the Game Boy.

By the latter half of the 1980s, when development on the Game Boy was well and truly underway, mass production of color LCD displays had begun, and pocket-sized color TVs were entering the marketplace. From a strictly technological standpoint, it would have been possible to create a portable color NES. But from the very beginning, Yokoi showed no interest in a color display and opted to use seasoned technology, the grayscale display.

What he was determined to create was a version of Game & Watch that had interchangeable games. It had to be small and light, and make efficient use of battery power. It would be durable, and playable in full sunlight—all features common to the Game & Watch series.

A color display did not reflect ambient light but instead relied on a backlight to illuminate its display. That made it larger, and significantly increased its power consumption. Even with a backlight, it was hard to ensure legibility in full sunlight. And most of all, the added cost did not justify its inclusion.

Yokoi was convinced that if the portable system were more expensive than the NES, consumers would pay it no mind. He was aiming for processing power equivalent to the NES. A machine equivalent to the NES with an LCD screen to boot wouldn't be cheap to begin with.

Yokoi was not so naive as to think that consumers would pay more than the price of an NES for a toy that went in their pocket. Color LCDs were still expensive, so from a cost perspective they were simply unfeasible for the new system.

Having explained to president Yamauchi that Color LCDs were a waste of battery power, were hard to see outside, and were too expensive, Yokoi got permission to move forward with a grayscale LCD, and with that the basic specifications were finalized.

Yet the cost barrier remained high.

No matter what they did, it seemed impossible to keep it below the price of the NES. The 160x144 LCD display was a particular problem—even if grayscale, it was expensive. And despite talks with Sharp—Nintendo's source for the LCD displays in the Game & Watch series—they were unable to agree on the price.

Game Boy development stalled, while elsewhere within the company, post-NES development surged forward.

Nintendo's domination would not last forever, and in the latter half of the 1980s, it was clear that they could not remain complacent. In 1987, NEC Home Electronics introduced the PC Engine (marketed in the US as the TurboGrafx-16) and the next year, Sega released the Mega Drive (or Genesis, as it was called in the US). The home console wars had begun.

Yamauchi had already directed R&D 2 to begin work on the successor to the NES. After the TurboGrafx-16 went on sale, the existence of the Super Famicom (or Super Nintendo Entertainment System, as it was dubbed in the US) was scooped by a local newspaper.

It was originally slated to hit the market in 1989, but a series of development delays meant that it didn't launch until November 1990, entering the market with Miyamoto's *Super Mario World*, among others.

The TurboGrafx, Genesis, and SNES that battled in the so-called "16-bit wars" all used 16-bit processors, with double the processing power found in the 8-bit NES. 16-bit processors hugely increased the number of colors and sounds the machines could reproduce.

In the end, the delays in the SNES's development only stoked the fires of fan enthusiasm, and the 16-bit wars ended with leading brand Nintendo's overwhelming victory, but Yokoi only watched from the sidelines. His low-tech approach was open to ridicule as anachronistic, but he never abandoned it.

The turning point for Yokoi and R&D 1 came when they were disassembling an LCD television that electronics maker Citizen had manufactured.

Circuit paths had been directly etched on the back of the LCD using a technique called "chip-on-glass," which simplified manufacturing and lowered costs significantly. After repeated negotiation visits to Citizen by Yokoi and others, the realization of the Game Boy was in sight.

But on the day Citizen personnel came to Nintendo to negotiate the last bits, Yokoi, seeing them out, espied a group from Sharp—who'd been thus far unable to meet their cost requirements for LCDs—entering the president's office. Yokoi slipped in with them, and when he returned to R&D 1, he announced, "Sharp says they can do it for the same price as Citizen, so we're going with Sharp."

The members of R&D 1 had no idea what had happened, but in any case, the price problem had been cleared, and Yokoi had given Sharp the green light. "Maybe Yokoi felt some obligation to Sharp after having worked with them for Game & Watch," people who knew him them muse.

With the go-ahead from Yokoi, a manager at the now world-famous Nintendo, Sharp augmented its production capacity with an investment of around 4 billion yen—but trouble awaited, in a development Yokoi would call "the worst failure of my life."

Yokoi had Sharp move ahead on the assumption that he would get the same type of TN (twisted nematic) LCD displays he'd used with Game & Watch. The displays were most optimally visible when viewed from a low diagonal angle, which had posed no problem for Game & Watch.

In *Yokoi Game House*, Yokoi recalls the moment he showed the much-awaited first prototype to Yamauchi:

> When I showed the prototype to the president, all he said was, "What the hell is this? I can't see a damn thing." And it was true, if you looked at the screen straight-on, it was hard to see. "What're you thinking? No one's gonna buy a game they can't see. Forget it." I was devastated.

The Game Boy used a portrait-type orientation, with the screen above the player's hands on the unit. Holding it like the Game & Watch units—at the optimal, low-diagonal viewing angle—resulted in glare from ambient light sources, but tilting it so that the screen directly faced the player ruined the LCD contrast. Yokoi had never noticed the flaw.

Production would have to be canceled. Yokoi trembled under the weight of the 4 billion yen investment Sharp had already made.

Upon consulting with the Sharp liaison, however, Yokoi was introduced to the new STN (super-twisted nematic) LCDs, and it seemed hope was on the horizon. They offered much better contrast at perpendicular viewing angles, but suffered from blurry afterimages when displaying rapid screen movement. Still, there was no choice but to try and use them. Feeling like he was grasping at straws, he sought Sharp's support for the next prototype.

In a marketplace ruled by high technology, and facing skepticism from within his own company, Yokoi had stubbornly bet on his own low-tech ideals. But now his own mistake might doom the project entirely and cause his old ally Sharp significant trouble. For those few weeks, he was so depressed he could hardly eat.

But Yokoi's passion moved the Sharp engineering staff. They tuned the STN LCD contrast for optimum balance so that the afterimages were no longer bothersome while the contrast was still good.

Yokoi hurried to show the new prototype to Yamauchi, whose casual response was "This'll do." In April 1989, the Game Boy finally made it to the marketplace, for 12,800 yen—2,000 yen cheaper than the NES.

The Game Boy was not hailed as particularly forward-thinking by the media. Its screen could only display four monotone levels, and it used four AA batteries. It generated the same beep-bloop sounds as the NES through a single monaural speaker. Yet Yokoi's faith in the Game Boy was absolute. It was the embodiment of the philosophy he'd developed at Nintendo.

The display visibility, which had once teetered on the brink of disaster, was hugely improved precisely because of that crisis. It could run for 35 hours on four AA batteries—playing two hours a day would give players over two weeks between battery changes.

It was built tough, with children dropping it in mind. The prototype presented to Yamauchi had survived being hurled at the carpet.

The Game Boy could play NES-style interchangeable games anywhere, and connecting two units with a cable let players challenge their friends. That alone was sufficiently fun for children. Even if a graphically superior competitor were to emerge, it wouldn't matter.

"Is yours black and white?" challenged Sega's commercial. Their portable console, the Game Gear, was released in October 1990 and used a backlit color LCD display. It could display 4,096 colors—more even than the NES. An optional peripheral turned it into a portable TV.

But the result for Sega was only failure. The Game Gear required six AA batteries and drained them in two or three hours. The screen was barely visible in sunlight, and hardly anyone was willing to carry the unit around—it was almost as big as a lunch box and weighed half a kilogram.

On the other hand, helped by hit games like *Tetris* and the *Pokémon* series, the Game Boy became ubiquitous worldwide. By 2000, 12 years after its release, worldwide sales totaled over 100 million units.

It's not color palettes, graphic quality, or hi-fi sound that make a game system fun.

Belief in that principle turned the Game Boy into a triumph.

Even after its development ended and the company turned its attention to the N64, Yokoi himself never strayed from his conviction. Before Iwata or Miyamoto, he had realized the truth of the "gaming crisis" and had taken appropriate action.

Ignoring the Cutting Edge

As you gaze into a large binocular-like device, a three-dimensional scene appears in vivid red, against a pitch-black background—the expanse of a pinball board, for example, or a *Mario* game. The ball or character moves towards you or away from you with a surprising illusion of depth.

In 1995, Nintendo introduced a 3-D game system dubbed the Virtual Boy. It had been developed by the Yokoi-led R&D 1 and was the last project at Nintendo Yokoi would be involved with.

It was the world's first 3-D game system, and an entirely Yokoi-like project—that is to say, it was the antithesis of the performance battles that were unfolding alongside it.

The SNES's dominance of the 16-bit war became clear by the mid-1990s, as the battlefield moved to 32-bit. The strongest contender was Sony's PlayStation.

As previously discussed, Nintendo's answer to the PlayStation was the supercomputer-like N64, released in 1996. It was around then that Yokoi was working on his own project—another monochrome system.

At the time, the head-mounted display developed by US company Reflection Technology was just starting to become widespread for aviation maintenance and military applications. The Virtual Boy's development was sparked by this technology arriving at Nintendo.

Aviation maintenance manuals or battle tactics could be accessed with one eye while the other was left free. The device looked like a pair of glasses with a small device obscuring one lens; it had been developed for use in situations where the wearer had to be able to interact with both a display and the surrounding environment. The display itself was made up of a single row of tiny red LEDs. They switched on and off rapidly while oscillating up and down to create an image.

Yokoi thought about the technology's potential to create a 3-D game system. Two of the red LED image projectors could be linked to display images to the left and right eyes, which would interpret the parallax differences as a three-dimensional world.

The colors and gradations would be the same as the Game Boy: one color, four levels of brightness. The screen resolution would be 384x224, a bit better than the NES, which would keep the price low for a revolutionary device, around 15,000 yen.

There was a reason Yokoi was so fixated on this product. In his book, he explained it thus:

> In videogames, there is always an easy way out if you don't have any good ideas. That's what the CPU competition and color competition are about. But there wouldn't be companies like Nintendo anymore who make games in their essence. Eventually those who're good at screen composition and CG would win, with Nintendo left with no place to stand. That's why I made the Virtual Boy—I wanted to make something that would bring us back to the essence of games.

From 8-bit to 16-bit, from 16 to 32... The images and sound became closer to reality every time. Game systems were designed to appeal to the hardcore fans and were leaving ordinary people behind.

To Yokoi, these kind of improvements were strictly superficial.

If Nintendo were to go down the same path, its days were numbered. The crisis that Iwata would come to sense so strongly in 2002 upon becoming president, Yokoi had felt in 1995 and taken action against. That action was the Virtual Boy.

Unfortunately, derided by the loudest hardcore gamers and ignored by fans who sought high-resolution graphics and convincing sound, the Virtual Boy faded without leaving a mark. Despite its red-monochrome display, the 3-D environments it was capable of depicting were surprisingly impressive, but they had to be experienced firsthand to be fully appreciated and were impossible to represent on the flat surface of a TV or magazine page. Demonstration units could only be experienced by one person at a time. The fact that publicity for the system couldn't convey the fun of playing it was a large factor in its failure.

The Virtual Boy ultimately sold 150,000 units in Japan, and 1.2

The 3-D gaming machine Virtual Boy, which went on sale in 1995, was the last original product Yokoi handled for Nintendo. The new guard of executives from Iwata and Miyamoto on down inherited the idea of pursuing "fun" and "surprise" rather than performance prowess. [Photo © Jiji]

million worldwide—the worst-performing system Nintendo ever made. Yet its significance for Nintendo is large relative to its poor sales performance.

In the debut issue of Japanese gaming magazine *Jugemu* in 1995, Yokoi said this:

> No matter how amazing the image you display on a TV screen, nobody's going to be surprised. But with stereoscopic vision, you can show them something with depth, and they'll discover something new nearly every day.

Iwata and Miyamoto realized the danger inherent to a game system that simply adhered to the technology roadmap, and instead pursued the true fun of games by creating the DS and Wii. Ten years after Yokoi, Nintendo's new management inherited his vision. Even now, Miyamoto calls him "my master": "Looking at some component and wondering what kind of product it might make, the way Yokoi used to—it's remained a basic part of our company culture. He always had that sense that going for the cutting edge isn't the only answer. Still, there's that fear of abandoning the cutting edge, especially when you're confronted by it in every game magazine and game expo. But our culture is such that when we start talking basics, it's like, yeah, Nintendo-ness is not going for the tech edge."

The kind of fun and surprise Yokoi wanted to present could not be expressed solely by relying on hardware performance. Of the roughly 70 games in the Game & Watch series, Yokoi had a hand in the conception and implementation of nearly all of them.

He was also responsible for many Game Boy titles.

"Yokoi's concentration when he was bent on making a fun game was tremendous," says Yoshihiro Taki, one of his subordinates at the time. For example, one of his hits was a puzzle game called *Dr. Mario*, which took its inspiration from the massively successful Russian game, *Tetris*.

Tetris debuted at the height of the NES's success, when side-scrolling action games like *Super Mario Bros.* and role-playing games like *Dragon Quest* were at their most popular. *Tetris*, a simple game in which the player arranges blocks that fall from the top of the screen to make them disappear, took Japan by storm, with children and adults alike becoming obsessed with the game.

The game was already popular at the arcades, but Nintendo quickly ported it to the Game Boy, causing the game's popularity to explode. The Game Boy version of *Tetris* sold over 4 million copies and contributed significantly to the platform's adoption—not unlike what *Brain Age* would do for the DS later.

Naturally, game creators across Japan were soon hard at work trying to figure out how to make a puzzle game to follow *Tetris*. Yokoi was one of them.

Perhaps it was the pure simplicity of the game, its basic fun, that excited him so. He played *Tetris* from dawn 'til dusk for a month, trying to think of a new game.

The game he finally produced, *Dr. Mario*, involved matching the colors of falling capsules to clear them, rather than the interlocking shapes of *Tetris*. It was Nintendo's first original puzzle game, and among the many post-*Tetris* contenders, it enjoyed the greatest longevity.

Dr. Mario's Game Boy version sold 2 million copies, and the NES version moved over 1.5 million, with sequels and spin-offs keeping the series alive. It perfectly embodied Yokoi's answer to the high-tech game system wars and software that chose to compete on the level of graphics and sound.

In August 1996, Yokoi retired from Nintendo at the age of 54, and a month later he founded Koto, a small toy company, in Kyoto.

At the time, there were whispered speculations that he had left Nintendo to take responsibility for the Virtual Boy's failure, or that there had been a fight with Yamauchi, but Taki—who was there to see—says none of this is true.

Yokoi had originally decided to retire at 50 to do as he pleased. His retirement had simply been a bit later than planned.

Beginning with Game & Watch and continuing on with the NES and SNES, Nintendo had grown from a simple playing card manufacturer to a world-famous videogame enterprise.

During that span, Yokoi—as manager of his friendly neighborhood R&D department section—had become gradually responsible for greater and greater earnings. There was always some discrepancy between what he wanted to do and what was profitable, and as the gap widened, Yokoi was increasingly uncomfortable. He wanted to do as he pleased—like back in the days when he created the Love Tester just to hold girls' hands.

The things he wanted to do were thoroughly outlined in the book he published shortly after retiring:

> —I want to try to create something new, by reconciling the world of real things with my world of play.
>
> —Something in the medical field might be interesting. During the development of the Virtual Boy, I had the opportunity to talk to medical professionals while working on product liability issues. We had some very good conversations about how elements from videogames might work themselves into physical therapy.
>
> —I want to think about how to bring the fun of games into real-world situations, like the medical field. Call it lateral thinking with seasoned videogames! (laugh)

On October 4, 1997, a year and a month after Koto's founding, Yokoi was involved in an automobile accident on the Hokuriku Expressway. He passed away. To say he hadn't finished all he hoped doesn't come close to the truth—he'd only just gotten his fresh start.

Crisis, amusement, surprise, delight, hardiness, seasoned technology, lateral thinking…

All of these keywords, so important to Iwata and Miyamoto, that revived "Nintendo the Game Maker," are linked to Yokoi, the products he created and the philosophy he espoused.

With games like *Brain Age* and *Wii Fit*, Iwata and Miyamoto vindicated Yokoi's ideas, applying Nintendo's strengths as an amusement shop to new fields and finding great success there.

If Nintendo does indeed have something like DNA, then it's no exaggeration to say that Yokoi is responsible for laying a large part of its foundation. His influence on Nintendo was huge.

But there is another person who cannot be forgotten.

That's none other than Yamauchi, who gave Yokoi his chance, who groomed Miyamoto, and who discovered his own successor in Iwata. Iwata, Miyamoto, Yokoi—tracing back that lineage, Yamauchi's presence looms large.

"They weren't boss and employee. They were father and son, it seemed to me," says an employee familiar with Yamauchi and Yokoi's relationship. Indeed, the two often interacted on the level of family; it was not rare for the Yamauchis and Yokois to have dinner together. What kind of father, then, was Yamauchi? What ideas did he hold and impart?

We cannot discuss Nintendo without meeting the man.

6

Surviving on Software

"What did Hiroshi Yamauchi care about? He couldn't stand making the same kind of toy the other guy was making, so whatever you showed him, you knew he was going to ask, 'How is this different from what everybody else is doing?' The worst way to answer was to tell him, 'It's not different, it's just a little better.' He'd be furious. He was very clear on just how foolish that attitude was for a toy company."

—Iwata

Yamauchi: Charisma and Intuition in Management

Not far from Kyoto's Shogoin temple, headquarters of the Yamabushi mountain ascetics, the richest man in Japan is in fine health.

Head up the narrow lane, barely wide enough for a single car to pass, and you will come to a gate set in a long wall. Pass through it, and you will see a large mansion in the Japanese style. The grand entryway to the building recalls a high-class traditional inn, and in it is displayed, among other curios, a woodblock print of the word "taiki" (roughly, "person of caliber"). Continuing on into the reception room, the view of the garden is like a microcosm of autumn in Kyoto. The trees in the meticulously-groomed courtyard are aflame with fall color; the scene is difficult to convey in words.

In the winter of 2007, the master of the house appeared there in the reception room, his stride confident. He was Hiroshi Yamauchi, the third president of Nintendo and the man who rebuilt the company he inherited.

In May 2002, he named the young Satoru Iwata as his successor and retreated to an advisory role. Since then, he has lived out his retirement at his home near Shogoin temple.

"I've quit Nintendo, you see. It would be odd for the guy who *used* to be the president to talk about the company, don't you think? Now that I've quit, I've got to leave the talking to the people who are still there," Yamauchi has frequently said ever since he retired, declining to be interviewed at all. But his perception is still keen. He still receives faxes regarding important issues regarding the business, and he holds tremendous influence over Nintendo's executives, beginning with Iwata.

Despite his retirement, he remains Nintendo's charismatic leader.

Yamauchi's charisma comes from his inimitable intuition. Iwata— whose strategy meetings and presentations are rife with data—has this to say: "He really is amazing. His instincts are incredibly keen, and he asks these piercing questions—you think to yourself, how did he know? I talk to him every so often on the phone, and it's like he could come back tomorrow and be the president without any trouble, he's that sharp. I need to vye against him some other way."

Yamauchi is an anomaly. He is not a pure lover of videogames like Iwata, nor is he a natural-born game creator like Miyamoto or Yokoi. During his tenure at Nintendo, he dealt with game systems only to make management decisions—he did not play more than he had to.

Since his retirement, while he fully understands the DS and the Wii, he plays neither. Nevertheless, his sense for what makes a hit is unparalleled, and he would occasionally give development teams hints that bordered on the clairvoyant.

"Can we make one with two games at once?" said Yamauchi to Yokoi, regarding the follow-up to 1980's Game & Watch. Yamauchi's word was law, but the LCD displays of the Game & Watch games weren't like the general-purpose LCDs of today—they were pre-printed with the graphics for a particular game. Getting two games on a single screen would be both difficult and expensive.

So Yokoi instead developed *Oil Panic*, the first in the "Multi-Screen" series of Game & Watch games. A single unit included two screens, which was akin to having two games. This would lead directly to the biggest hit in the entire Game & Watch series: *Donkey Kong*.

As discussed in the first chapter of this book, another twin-screened game machine, the DS, arose from Yamauchi's advice. When he retired in 2002, he entrusted his successors with the concept of two displays. Iwata and Miyamoto took that idea and ultimately turned it into the touch screen-equipped DS.

Even the Game Boy, which supported Nintendo through the years when the company's home console business was foundering, benefitted from Yamauchi's criticism. It was at his behest that the LCD display was improved, which helped turn it into a huge hit, unchallenged by competitors' color screens whose outdoor visibility was poor.

And it was keen intuition indeed that led him to prdouce the Game & Watch series in the first place. It thrust Nintendo into the videogame industry.

The fateful day that decision was made, Yamauchi had a meeting to attend, but his driver was absent. With a sudden need for someone to drive his Cadillac, he turned to Yokoi, who himself drove a foreign car. "I had to think of something work-related to talk about in the car," said Yokoi in his memoir. "So I told him about the bored-looking salaryman on the bullet train."

At the time, all Yamauchi did was nod thoughtfully; "Mm, mm," he said. But when he arrived at the meeting, the then-president of Sharp, Akira Saeki, happened to be in attendance. Yamauchi brought up the idea of a calculator-based game, and from there development on Game & Watch began in earnest.

Yamauchi was not particularly good with electronics, nor was he a game specialist. Nevertheless, he made the important snap decisions that took Nintendo from being a Kyoto playing card manufacturer to a world-straddling videogame giant.

His casual statements, one by one, led to the incredible successes that followed.

As those successes began to mount, they magnified his charisma. Eventually Nintendo employees took his words to be absolute, almost oracular in nature.

Yamauchi's decisions sometimes put strain on the workplace, causing friction with the staff, but as a member of the founding family and the largest stockholder, he enjoyed absolute authority. When he said to turn right, the company turned right.

To put it favorably, he was a disciplined president; a less generous term might be "autocratic"—but call it what you may, it is what made Nintendo the company it is today.

After the success of Game & Watch, Yamauchi paid off the debt Nintendo had assumed, then unhesitatingly put the remaining funds towards the NES. A project to develop arcade-style game machines was grinding along, but Yamauchi canceled it, concentrating on the NES.

Miyamoto looks back on that era: "I was working on the arcade

His eye for hits peerless, Advisor Yamauchi continues to be fearsomely suggestive to the crew. [Photo © Jij]

project when work started on the NES—me and Takeda both were. But then Yamauchi said 'No more arcade machines' and shifted the entire arcade team to the NES project. It was like he just closed up the company. I remember thinking at the time, 'Is that really a good idea?'"

The company Miyamoto refers to is Nintendo Leisure System, established in 1973 to handle sales and maintenance of arcade game systems. Properly speaking, it was reabsorbed into Nintendo after the release of the NES. At the time, the *Donkey Kong* arcade machine was proving successful, so Miyamoto's surprise was understandable.

But in the end, it was a brilliant decision. Iwata elaborates: "The speed of the decision meant that Nintendo quickly took the number one spot in home consoles. He had to be autocratic to make such a reckless decision." He continues, "It's because Yamauchi made the best decisions given the constraints, limited resources, and market conditions of the time that Nintendo was able to grow from a small playing card maker to what it is today. If you told me to do the same thing, I'm not at all sure I could pull it off."

Yokoi also acknowledged Yamauchi-the-gambler's ability. As discussed previously, when Yokoi left the company, rumors about the circumstances of his departure circulated through the game industry and media. He'd gotten tired of Yamauchi's unilateral, overbearing style, the gossip went.

But in an article on his reasons for leaving Nintendo that ran in the November 1996 issue of news magazine *Bungei Shunju*, Yokoi put those rumors to rest, writing, "I think Nintendo has achieved what it has thanks to his unilateral style." While voices within the company had been skeptical regarding the development of Game & Watch, Yokoi noted, Yamauchi pushed the project through to productization, turning billions of yen of debt into billions of yen in cash.

Moreover, he then poured that money back into the NES and created another hit; it was another bold move from Yamauchi. Yokoi knew that the advances Nintendo had made were inextricably tied to Yamauchi's autocratic methods.

Progression of Nintendo's Business Performance (1980-2001)

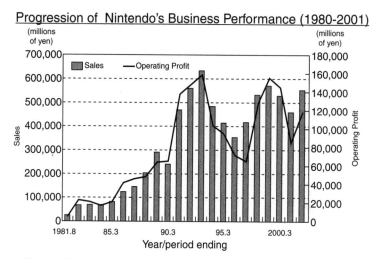

Note: For 1981 only, period ended in August.

In 1980 (specifically, the fiscal year ending August 1981) Nintendo's sales totaled 23 billion yen, with operating profits at 4.3 billion yen. Then came Game & Watch, the NES, the Game Boy, the SNES—and in 1992 (the fiscal year ending March 1993) sales had ballooned to 634.5 billion yen, with operating profits rising to 159.2 billion.

In just 12 years, Yamauchi had grown sales by a factor of 27, with operating profits 37 times what they had been previously.

But this highly improbable growth would not last.

They would meet with fierce competition from Sony in the home console market, and by 1995 sales and operating profits fell to 354.2 billion and 71.9 billion, respectively. Though their results in following years would be buoyed by the continuing success of the Game Boy and *Pokémon* series, they did not again reach the heights of 1992.

Just before Yamauchi retired in May 2002, 2001 sales and profits were 554.8 billion and 119.1 billion yen.

But Yamauchi the gambler was not quite finished.

He regrouped and placed his bets on the next generation. Given the unprecedented profits his bet yielded, one has to admit—his clairvoyance is incredible.

153

One Last Bet on the Next Generation

In May 2002, at the age of 74, Yamauchi decided to retire.

Looking back on his decision, he has this to say: "If I had some kind of guarantee that I could stay healthy forever, then I doubt I would've retired. But that's not how it goes, so I had to choose a time. No one was going to tell me to quit, so I had to make the decision on my own."

He had been with Nintendo for 52 years. The charismatic man that had taken the company to the world stage was declining in health and vigor. But no one—not outside the company, and certainly not within it—would suggest that he retire. He talked about retiring at the beginning of the 21st century and, having discovered a successor in Iwata, made his decision.

But there remained something to do.

For Yamauchi, the transition of the presidency did not just mean his retirement. It was also his last great challenge, to sow the seeds of Nintendo's next success with the coming generation of leadership.

Iwata explains. "Yamauchi was probably the first to start proselytizing that the videogame industry was not healthy. Being separated from the rank-and-file gave him a commanding view, and he surely has a special talent for seeing things—he was much quicker than we were to realize that things couldn't continue as they were."

Games were becoming denser both graphically and sonically; their production was becoming larger and more industrial. If a game was a hit, it would get any number of sequels. Yokoi was the first to articulate the danger inherent in this path—but he died in a traffic accident in 1997, shortly after leaving Nintendo to pursue his solution to this problem. As if to carry on his legacy, Yamauchi loudly and forcefully argued Yokoi's position within the industry.

In September 1999, at a partnership press conference with game giant Konami, he said this: "The game software industry is reaching a turning point. If we continue to pursue this kind of large-scale software development, costs will pile up and it will no longer be a viable business."

The next September, at a briefing with industry analysts, he had this to say: "Large-scale games are no good. If we keep it up, game makers the world over are going to collapse. These industrial-strength games are played out. The true nature of the videogame business is developing new kinds of fun and constantly working to achieve perfection."

The videogame world had run out of ideas and ways to surprise players. The easy way out—making games bigger and louder—would eventually drive customers away, and the entire industry would sink.

Yamauchi's prediction agreed with the reality that Iwata faced. Yamauchi had even foreseen the phenomenon of players leaving games behind—the same phenomenon that ultimately inspired the mainstreaming strategy Nintendo would pursue.

Unfortunately, Yamauchi's foresight wasn't turned into concrete strategy right away—it was only after Iwata's ascent that mainstream-friendly products like the DS, Wii, and *Brain Age* became reality. Put another way, the company was unable to respond to Yamauchi.

Yamauchi was not the kind of leader that took on projects on his own and descended into the company to see them executed.

He instead found people like Yokoi, gave them strategic direction, made executive decisions, and occasionally offered his opinions. No one could object to him, but because his indications always resulted in fun products, he acquired charisma to spare.

But the two generations of home consoles that followed the SNES—the 64 and the GameCube—ended up being misses. The new portable consoles were merely updated versions of Yokoi's original design, lacking fresh ideas, and there were no revolutionary mega-hits on the platform outside of the *Pokémon* series.

The management style had to change. Perhaps that was the true reason for Yamauchi's retirement.

The man he appointed as his successor, Iwata, was familiar enough with the nuts and bolts of game creation that he had written code himself. He wouldn't have to make unilateral decisions—he could work collaboratively, convincing the people around him of his ideas, communicating all the way down the management chain. He was the antithesis of Yamauchi.

Because this was the case, Yamauchi hedged his bets against drastic change while seeing hope in Iwata's new style of management.

"From a single charismatic leader to a group management policy"—so went the media reports when the presidency change was announced in May 2002. Iwata was the president. Miyamoto was in charge of software. Takeda was the hardware man. All three of them, plus three others, were granted representative power.

Says Iwata, "What troubles might a company have after a charismatic leader retires? The main issue would be keeping it unified, avoiding factionalism, having a way to bring different outlooks together. The structure Yamauchi put in place is still functioning really well. You have to give it to him!"

Offsetting the risk of a drastic reversal in management style represented Yamauchi's last great challenge. The odds were in his favor. Yamauchi explains: "Around the time I retired, I was thinking it was time to do a handheld system with two screens. The problem was how to develop the idea and flesh it out. I decided to leave it to the new guys. Fortunately, Nintendo had some room to maneuver. There was no debt and plenty of savings, so it wasn't going to collapse because of something minor. On the one hand, we were losing to Sony which had put us in a bad spot, and on the other hand I was leaving the success of the two-screened system to a new gang. If they couldn't make it go, it just meant they were no good as Nintendo executives."

He'd given them the idea of two screens. If that wasn't enough, nothing could be done. It was the noble gambler's last bet—and it paid off magnificently. Sales rose to a stunning 1.2 trillion yen, with operating profit at 400 billion yen.

It was a final display of intuition and daring from Yamauchi, and it was rooted in an inarguable principle.

Software Leads, Hardware Follows

Why did Yamauchi pick Iwata? You can chalk it up to intuition, but it was still one of the things your correspondent most wanted to ask him about.

His answer: "If you want to know how Nintendo picks people, it's about having a 'software orientation.' When you talk to people, you can tell whether they're hardware types, or if they have affinity with software. I myself am more of a software-oriented executive, so I think I can probably tell that sort of thing."

During the interview, Yamauchi used the term "software orientation" many times. It applies to more than personnel selection. Yamauchi's entire management philosophy is predicated on this idea of software orientation.

In Yamauchi's view, industry is largely divisible into hardware and software. Automobiles, steel, shipbuilding, home electronics—it goes without saying that all of these manufacturing-based enterprises deal with hardware, and that the products they create are necessary to make our lives longer and better.

Manufacturing equals hardware equals daily necessities. Corporations in this category survive by making better, cheaper products.

They work tirelessly to advance the state of the art while simultaneously seeking cheaper sources of labor, taking advantage of the efficiencies of large scale to make our lives more convenient.

As a result, there is a rise in demand for ways to have more fun, ways to use our free time, ways to make our lives more satisfying—and thus the amusement industry emerges.

This industry is different in every way from the industries that supply daily necessities.

Because they do not deal with products that people need, they must offer experiences that are fun, surprising, and easy-to-engage—otherwise no one will spare them any attention. It is an industry not of technology, performance, and price, but of fun and games—in other words, software.

Put another way, it's Yamauchi's view that the amusement industry is not a hardware business focused on creating better-performing, cheaper products, but a software-oriented industry where polished content is the goal.

Nintendo is a corporation fully committed to the amusement business, so this orientation is deeply ingrained.

According to Yamauchi, the fact that Nintendo has emerged victorious during the recent ravages of capitalism and the market stands as proof that the top executive was able to maintain the orientation. "If I were a hardware-oriented executive, I don't think Nintendo could ever have gotten this far. The DS and the Wii, and the NES before that—people have come to call them huge hits thanks to our software orientation. If Nintendo had a hardware-oriented executive, I'd have to ask him to quit. Otherwise, Nintendo would go bankrupt."

Just as Yamauchi says, it was when Nintendo started to put their strength in software to use that its fortunes changed.

The extending lattice-arm hit toy that was Ultra Hand came from Yamauchi telling Yokoi to "make a game out of" his invention, which was dutifully followed up by the addition of a grasping mechanism.

When the NES went on sale, Nintendo carefully controlled the circulation of its software. Nintendo commissioned the manufacture of all of the cartridges, even for games created by outside developers. They had absolute authority over software, including whether or not a given game would even be put on market.

That was because Yamauchi didn't see selling the hardware as the core of the NES business—it was built on selling the games that ran on that hardware. In order to prevent a glut of cheap, badly written games, they maintained standards for fun and quality.

When Nintendo abandoned its software orientation and turned to hardware, its fortunes inevitably declined. The 64, with its incredible computer power that was nonetheless difficult to create games for, is the perfect example of this.

Yamauchi reflects. "We have many hardware-oriented employees, but they can't just be fired, can they? At the time of the NES we were blessed with software types, but there were new developers involved when it came to the 64. And unfortunately, they weren't software-oriented. That's why they made something like the 64. I was dissatisfied. 'Nintendo's in trouble,' I thought, when the 64 was released."

Yet Nintendo hardly neglects the performance and engineering of a game system's hardware. A game's ability to be appealing is supported by the capabilities of the hardware on which it runs, after all. But the software is the main axis, and the software must be given priority. That is the software orientation that Yamauchi talks about.

"Our business is one where hardware and software come together. We can't talk about software without knowing about hardware. But the question is what then to do with that knowledge. For example, Sony is a company where hardware leads, and software follows. Nintendo is the opposite—software leads, and hardware follows. But Nintendo understands hardware. I'm confident that that won't change," says Yamauchi. He has chanted this lesson like a mantra to Iwata, Miyamoto, and other successors. And his teachings do not stop there.

Be Devoted to Play, Be Original

As stated previously, Nintendo does not have a formally written mission statement or guiding principle. Yamauchi explains: "I hate the term 'corporate philosophy,' so I'm opposed to articulating that kind of thing. But the number of managers where you can't tell whether they're managers or pundits is increasing, and so is the number of books by people like that. But what's the point of reading them? Maybe for reference, but I don't think you can become a successful manager that way. That's something you have to figure out for yourself, which is why I don't use those terms. Although of course without any ideas at all, you can't manage anything."

These ideas of Yamauchi's were delivered verbally to his successors, Iwata and others—he told his disciples everything they would need to create "Nintendo-ness."

During the Q&A of a corporate strategy briefing in October 2008, Iwata related the following anecdote.

"The six of us lined up here are all Hiroshi Yamauchi's pupils. What did Hiroshi Yamauchi care about? He couldn't stand making the same kind of toy the other guy was making, so whatever you showed him, you knew he was going to ask, 'How is this different from what everybody else is doing?' The worst way to answer was to tell him, 'It's not different, it's just a little better.' He'd be furious. He was very clear on just how foolish that attitude was for a toy company. So in that sense, 'Do something different from the other guy!' is deeply engrained in our DNA."

Yamauchi took every opportunity to impart wisdom to his protégés. The basis of his lessons was "maintaining a software orientation," and various other teachings derived from that foundation are writ large on Iwata and others' hearts.

Maintaining a software orientation is synonymous with being devoted to fun. It's precisely because Nintendo limits its business to amusement that it cannot afford to do the same things as its competitors. An amusement company lives and dies by its ability to surprise and delight its customers.

Yamauchi repeated these ideas to Iwata, Miyamoto, and the rest. He impressed upon them the severity that is ironically imposed on an amusement company. Says Iwata, "The number one thing that Yamauchi beat into us was an understanding of the distinction between an appliance product and an amusement product."

The ease and responsiveness of a user interface, the need for intuitive controls and physical hardiness, the importance of customer support—the elements through which Iwata says Nintendo's strengths as a game company were most effectively expressed were the same elements Yamauchi taught him to distinguish.

Remaining humble despite immense success and not forgetting they're "just a toy maker" is another stance underwritten by Yamauchi's teachings. One of his disciples, Miyamoto, explains. "Yamauchi was always telling me 'know your limits.' He hated hubris above all else. There's a fine line between confidence and overconfidence, but he was incredibly sensitive to it. That's why he told us to think of the whole company as a person, and to look at it objectively. He was very admonishing about this, and I think I've learned a lot there."

Even after his retirement, Yamauchi's teachings are occasionally conveyed to Iwata and company, functioning as reminders to the executives.

E3 2006—the debut of the Wii, which would go on sale that December. Nintendo's follow-up to the DS met with rave reviews for the console and praise for the company.

Iwata immediately reported the good response to Yamauchi. "It's true, you've got to be at least this unique," said Yamauchi in praise of the new console, but immediately qualified the statement. "But don't think that the Wii is going to succeed just because the DS did."

"The good reception at E3 made the whole company exuberant for a moment," says Iwata, looking back. "But soon Takeda was saying 'It's not over yet,' and I was telling people, 'Making people smile for five minutes at an event is one thing, selling the product and making it fly is another matter.' Yamauchi's lessons and our attitudes were the same, and that was good. I was glad it wasn't like he was throwing cold water on us while we on our part were unthinkingly exuberant."

Be devoted to play. Be original. Understand the difference between appliances and toys. Know your limits. Yamauchi's words shaped Nintendo's corporate culture, having been passed from him down to Iwata and beyond. So why haven't they still been written down, codified into a mission statement and shared with the whole company?

Just as Yamauchi says, it is because he hates the term "corporate philosophy" and believes that any executive who needs it written down will never achieve greatness.

Here Iwata has his own interpretation. "Nintendoism means not having a corporate philosophy, a mission statement. If you're always following a mission statement, your customers are going to get bored with you."

Don't do what the other guy is doing. Doing the same thing over and over again bores people. Be flexible in face of changes in the environment. Don't assume that past success implies future success.

According to Iwata, it's impossible to both be original and hew to a codified policy.

Yamauchi's teachings have spawned new interpretations from his pupils as Nintendo-ness continues to evolve—but even as it evolves, Yamauchi's students hold his precepts near to their hearts, always minding them. Thus, even as Nintendo stays flexible, changing in response to its environment, its core is unwavering.

Nintendo exists because of Yamauchi; its strengths come from his ideas and lessons.

But no charismatic leader could establish these theories in a single day. It was only through overcoming many failures and difficulties that Yamauchi deepened his resolve to be a mere toy maker and learned how to survive as such.

7

From Playing Cards to the World Stage

"In our business, if you succeed it's like you've gone to heaven, but failure is like falling to hell. So whether or not a great concept comes up—it's all about the ideas."

—*Yamauchi*

The Young Master From Kyoto

Ten-odd minutes' walk southwest from Nintendo's headquarters in the Kamitoba district of Kyoto are the main offices of the Minami Yasaka Taxi company. Its parent company is the Yasaka Group, whose green three-leaf clover is a common sight in the Kyoto region. Minami Yasaka Taxi employs 150 people and has a fleet of 84 cars.

The company's headquarters are still in the same brown four-story building in which it was founded, and on the roof of that building can be seen a different logo, a rhombus—the one for Daiya (Diamond) Taxi, which was the company's name at the time of its founding.

Not many people know that Daiya Taxi was originally a subsidiary of Nintendo.

Taxis, foodstuffs, photocopiers… There was once a time when Nintendo was diversified in ways that are unimaginable now. It took on debt and teetered on the edge of bankruptcy.

And throughout all those trials, Yamauchi's instincts were being honed, preparing him to steer Nintendo through to its future as a game company.

Yamauchi is the great-grandson of Fusajiro Yamauchi, the first president of Nintendo. Fusajiro was not blessed with a son, so he adopted, via marriage to his daughter, the man who would become the next president of the company, Sekiryo Yamauchi. Like his father-in-law, Sekiryo also had no son, and adopted artisan Shikanojo Inaba by arranging a marriage with his eldest daughter. Yamauchi was the oldest son of Shikanojo, and he took his place in Kyoto as the heir of an expectant Yamauchi family in November 1927.

Although Shikanojo soon abandoned the family, his parents—Yamauchi's grandparents—raised their heir in comfort, grooming him for his future. Shortly after the end of the war, he announced that he wanted to go enjoy himself in Tokyo. He moved there and enrolled in the law program at Waseda University.

The "young master from Kyoto" lived it up in Tokyo. He had a house that his grandfather purchased for him in Tokyo's Shibuya district, where he lived with friends. It was an exclusive district that housed (among others) commissioned officers of the US occupation forces. He dined on beefsteak and wine—things the average citizen could never afford—and passed his days playing billiards. But in 1949, his fourth year of school, his rich-boy lifestyle changed when his grandfather Sekiryo, the second president of Nintendo, collapsed from illness.

The moment Yamauchi's father abandoned the family, Yamauchi's own future had been decided. He returned to Kyoto, where his dying grandfather charged him with the family and company's future. At the tender age of 22, he took control of Nintendo, stipulating that he be the only family member involved with the company—all others were to be excluded.

At the time, Nintendo's chief product was traditional *hanafuda* playing cards. The cards were almost hand-made—materials were delivered to hundreds of homes, where the cards were carefully made by people who did it as a sideline. Employees on bicycles would then ride around to collect the cards. "Who does this rich kid think he is?" thought many within the company. But Yamauchi paid them no mind as he set about modernizing his grandfather's company.

In 1951, he changed the company name from Yamauchi Nintendo to Nintendo Koppai—also read "karuta," a term, derived from Portuguese to refer to playing cards, that had entered the Japanese vocabulary centuries earlier via traders. Next, Yamauchi established a factory and plunged into automated manufacture. In 1953 Nintendo became the first Japanese company to produce plastic playing cards.

The plastic cards were resistant to stains and hard to bend. Nintendo steadily rode the wave of postwar economic recovery, and in 1959 they had another hit—licensed playing cards.

Like any playing cards, Nintendo's had the standard suits and numbers on one side, with geometric patterns on the backs—until they struck a deal with the Walt Disney company to sell cards with characters like Mickey Mouse on the card backs.

Given their associations with gambling, playing cards were generally regarded as an adult's plaything. But these character-printed cards were aimed at children and even included a "how to play" guide with rules for several games. They were a hit.

This was when Yamauchi first realized both the explosive potential in games and the importance of software—but he was not yet prepared to pursue that path.

Heaven If We Win, Hell If We Lose

Riding the success of the Disney playing cards, Nintendo Koppai went public in 1962, offering its stock on the Osaka and Kyoto Securities Exchanges. The next year the company's name changed again, this time to the current Nintendo Co., Ltd.

Nintendo had a fresh start and was brimming with energy. However, the efforts to move past playing cards into new businesses would lead to 20 years of suffering for the company.

Shortly after the Tokyo Olympics in 1964, the motorization of the nation was rapidly advancing; foreseeing this, Yamauchi's opening move had been to spin off a taxi company. Next he decided that the logical follow-up to the new instant ramen on the market would be instant rice, so he created a food company.

Perhaps trying to recapture the success of the Disney playing cards, in the mid-1960s Yamauchi developed a series of licensed items including "Disney *furikake*" (furikake is a mixture of dried seasonings to sprinkle over rice) and "Popeye ramen." A few years later he entered the office equipment market with simplified photocopiers and calculators.

But this was not so much diversification as it was deviation.

With Japan's rapid economic growth, the amusement market was becoming larger and more diverse as well. The once-strong sales of Disney playing cards shuddered to a halt. Later, Yamauchi would reflect on this era of Nintendo, saying, "We just didn't know what to do." They had been cornered into trying to diversify. The result was disaster.

Overlapping investments and products that didn't sell. Ballooning debt and inventory. With the company on the verge of collapse, Yamauchi was desperate to raise money. He managed to scrape by on steady sales of hanafuda and karuta cards. Then, in 1965, Nintendo hired the man who would go on to develop the toy ideas that saved the company—Yokoi.

Ultra Hand, Ultra Machine, Love Tester...

Yokoi's hit toys went from selling hundreds of thousands to millions of units. The toys, created from little more than simple hardware and clever concepts, nonetheless generated sufficient cash to right the listing Nintendo.

With Yokoi's use of lateral thinking on seasoned technologies, Nintendo turned in earnest toward electronic toys; the Ray Gun series is representative, and it grew into an unprecedented success.

Nintendo is an amusement company—and amusement depends on the software aspect.

The notion had been carved into Yamauchi's mind, and he set about preparing the company to follow the path of a game company. The taxi subsidiary and food subsidiaries were folded as Nintendo devoted itself to its new goal, but success would not come easily. They were about to undergo a difficult baptism.

The ray gun, while popular, was plagued with manufacturing defects; there were times when it would sell but profits would be negligible. Nonetheless Yamauchi saw through to a new era where toys of all kinds used electronics.

"Let's make some kind of competition out of our ray gun," he said to Yokoi.

At the time, the air gun boom was in full swing, and competitions involving air guns were becoming more common. In response to Yamauchi's directive, Yokoi devised a ray gun version of clay pigeon shooting, which he called "Laser Clay Pigeon," and in 1973, the first recreational facility to offer (in its own exaggerated words) "The world's first laser clay pigeon range!" opened in Kyoto. The building had previously been a bowling alley, but now at the far end of the lanes were large projection screens. As the clay pigeon arced across the screen, players would aim and fire at them with sensor-equipped shotguns. If a hit was registered, the clay pigeon would shatter.

It was extremely well-received. Press and customers flooded into the new establishments, and orders poured in from struggling bowling alleys nationwide. Nintendo ordered materials and parts at an unprecedented rate to keep pace with the development.

Yet what eventually shattered was not clay pigeons, but dreams—for 1973 was the year of the oil crisis.

Orders were canceled one after the other. The growth that had been projected for the fiscal year ending August 1974 failed to materialize; sales were actually down to 3.5 billion yen, with liabilities up to 5 billion. Nintendo had plunged from heaven into hell. The future was unknowable. Yamauchi had just turned 50, and he was on the verge of surrender—but Game & Watch would be the biggest hit in the company's history to date, not only breathing new life into the company but bringing in more than enough cash to wipe out their debt.

"In our business, if you succeed it's like you've gone to heaven, but failure is like falling to hell. So whether or not a great concept comes up—it's all about the ideas," says Yamauchi now. He has personally weathered wildly fluctuating fortunes in learning how to survive as a game company, and learned the importance of software. Yet at the same time, painful experience has demonstrated that the game world is a difficult one in which to live. Surviving in it has fostered in Nintendo the resolve to deliver delight and surprise, always distinguishing itself from its competitors.

Even worse, Yamauchi goes on to say, is that "thinking and thinking doesn't guarantee a good result. Sometimes it's better to go with a moment's flash of inspiration instead of spending years and years on an idea." And in fact, both the Ultra Hand and Game & Watch were developed based on snap decisions.

We do not live in a world where effort guarantees results. The ability to confidently seize moments of inspiration is critical for an executive. Iwata faithfully executed this lesson of Yamauchi's when he promptly put Miyamoto's idea to equip the DS with a touch screen into action.

Everything Yamauchi says is the result of what he's learned through long experience.

He learned something else, though—a lesson from a difficult period of Nintendo's history.

Composure in Failure, Humility in Triumph

Besides amusement and software orientation, at the heart of Nintendo's corporate culture is a deep respect for the importance of luck. No matter how huge their hits might be, they are careful to stay humble.

Yamauchi does not make big displays of his success as a manager. Instead, he talks about his own software orientation, and about his good luck. This holds true even when he discusses the eras of the 64 and GameCube, which were a dark time for Nintendo.

"I was lucky—we had the Game Boy, and then *Pokémon* came out. There were still software-oriented people at Nintendo, and they managed to offset the situation. Why was that? All I can say is that I was lucky."

To hear Yamauchi tell it, the success of the DS and Wii can be chalked up to luck, too.

"A new genre of games like *Brain Age* and *Shaberu! DS Oryori Navi* ("It talks! DS Cooking Navigator") came out and really helped the DS gain wider acceptance. The fact that these new types of software managed to bring in a new kind of user was fortunate for Nintendo, I say, and meaningful for Nintendo, because it would be strange to claim that we had planned for it to happen all along. Nobody is that smart."

His successors have certainly absorbed this lesson. In "The President Asks" series of interviews conducted by Iwata and published on the Nintendo webpage, Iwata says this:

To get the results you want, you need a measure of good

fortune. After all, just because you did the right thing doesn't mean everything will work out. That's true for what people are going to think is fun, but it's even more true for whether or a product is going to be a hit—there's always a large factor that you simply can't control.

The future is unknowable; luck is the purview of heaven—simply focus on doing your best at what you can do.

This is Yamauchi's explanation of what the characters in Nintendo's company name mean ("nin" = trust/leave to; "ten" = heaven). Both inside and outside the company, he's often adds to this, "Don't believe that saying, 'give your all and heaven will take care of the rest.' There is no all. There is no limit to effort." Yet he's also said, "There is fortune that no human effort could match." In other words, fortune will decide in the end—but you have to give your all until then.

When you're lucky, be grateful. When you're not, move on. A management style that respects the place of fortune, in other words, is constantly tranquil. Yamauchi, having learned to survive in the harsh world that is the game industry, avoids extremes of both joy and despair despite the ups and downs of business, and instead aims for a calm, balanced style of management.

"Composure in failure, humility in triumph"—Yamauchi's motto. When not favored by fortune, stay composed and work hard. When blessed with luck, remain humble and put forth your best effort. Yamauchi has told this to himself and to those who succeeded him.

Nintendo grew thanks to flashes of inspiration, but behind that, the company's disposition is calm and serious. That serenity comes from Yamauchi's experience.

Over half a century passed between when Yamauchi joined Nintendo and when he retired. His values, having survived countless difficulties, were distilled into the words "software orientation" and "fortune," and impressed upon the company.

It was not unlike the spirit of the generations of playing-card makers before him, stretching all the way back to the Muromachi era, centuries before.

The Enterprising Spirit of *Karuta* Craftsmen

In September 2009, Nintendo reached its 120th year since its founding.

A wood-block printer named Fusajiro Yamauchi established the company in September 1889, in the 22nd gloriously democratic year of the Empire of Japan's Meiji era.

120 years of tradition. But considering that *hanafuda* cards were created during the feudal Edo period, and *karuta* cards went back even further, to the Muromachi period, Nintendo's establishment seems like a relatively recent development.

Sanseido's *Daijirin* dictionary defines "karuta" thus: "Small, rectangular cards used for amusement or gambling. Alternatively, games played with such cards. Printed with letters or illustrations, a deck consists of many cards. Variants include poem karuta (*hyakunin isshu*), *iroha* karuta ("alphabet karuta"), flower karuta (hanafuda), and Western-style playing cards."

Karuta first reached Japan in the latter half of the 16th century, after the arrival of Portuguese traders on the island of Tanegashima opened up contact with Europe. Along with Western goods like furs and firearms, playing cards were introduced, and they became known as "karuta," after the Portuguese term.

Eventually, during the Taisei era (1573–1591), artisans on Kyushu began to produce imitations of these cards, and thus so-called "Taisei karuta" became the first domestically produced playing cards.

They were woodblock prints, with colorful Western-style illustrations. In place of the familiar suits like hearts or spades, they had 12 cards of swords, cups, coins, and staves, for a total of 48 cards to a deck, after the fashion of European cards of the time.

This strange new toy from the West grew steadily in popularity among the soldiers of the era, as a way of killing their considerable free time. Not long after, some of them began to use karuta to gamble.

One such instance came with Hideyoshi Toyotomi's invasion of

Korea in 1597, a campaign that involved 140,000 soldiers. The troops assembled from all over Japan at the headquarters in the province of Hizen (modern-day Saga prefecture), and there they learned of karuta. It was around this time that the feudal warlord of Tosa province outlawed the cards for the first time.

Karuta—so the reasoning went—weakened soldier morale and resolve and were a disruption to public morals.

Henceforth the history of karuta in Japan is the history of the ways in which the game slipped past the regulations placed on it by the government. No matter how oppressed karuta printers were, they were always clever enough to survive.

When Hideyoshi died and the Tokugawa clan claimed power, ushering in the Edo era, karuta production shifted from Kyushu to Kyoto, and adoption among the common folk spread. Gambling dens frequented mostly by *ronin* (masterless samurai) prospered, bringing with them the associated societal problems.

Both provincial administrations and the *bakufu* (unified feudal government) handed down proscription after proscription against gambling, but when they proved ineffective, the production of the cards themselves was banned. This put an end to the so-called *Tensho karuta*, named after the era in which it first prospered.

But the woodblock artisans would not so easily throw their craft away. The end of Tensho karuta brought with it the Edo era's *uta-garuta* ("poem karuta"). Uta-garuta was a matching game played with pairs of cards printed with either the opening or ending of a poem along with a portrait of the poet.

The poems were from famous collections like the *Kokinshu*, *Man'yoshu*, and *Hyakunin Isshu*—the last of which gives the game its modern name. Though the method of the cards' production was the same as before, the play and designs were distinct from the Western-inspired karuta that preceded them. To couch it in modern terms, they dealt with the new regulations by changing the software. Uta-garuta was a refined, elegant game. Not used for gambling, it was played by the elite. As the cards were used as an educational tool, or were simply collected as *objets d'art*, karuta artisans realized a new source of profit.

Edo artisans were an entrepreneurial lot. With the adoption of uta-garuta by the elite, they next trained their eyes on the commoners. Uta-garuta that drew on collections of classical poetry were difficult for commoners to play, as they lacked formal educations. But variants of the game that used common proverbs were much more accessible. Thus was born *iroha-garuta*, or "alphabet karuta."

Success in this business was glorious, but government regulation was frequent, and changes in fashion were extreme.

Perhaps it was out of awareness of this situation that the artisans of the chief karuta-production region, Kyoto, chose the proverb "*issunsaki wa yami*" ("darkness is only an inch away") as the matching card for the very first character "i" in the *iroha* system of arranging the Japanese syllabary. Parents and grandparents began purchasing sets of iroha-garuta for their children, for educational purposes, and it grew into an entirely different market from its predecessor, uta-garuta.

Meanwhile, there were other artisans who continued printing Tensho karuta in defiance of the proscriptions against it. They avoided the ban by using Japanese-style artwork in lieu of European pictures, and in the mid-Edo period, entering the 1700s, a new style of karuta began to appear: *unsun karuta*.

The cards might have depictions of the seven gods of fortune—Ebisu or Daikoku, say—and the number of cards in a deck rose to 75. Helped by the new game possibilities, unsun karuta became instantly popular among the common people. Since play drew on the Tensho karuta tradition, gambling soon followed. Under the mercantilist policies of Tanuma Okitsugu in the mid-1700s, restrictions were lax, and the cards reached a peak of popularity.

However, power shifted from Okitsugu to Sadanobu Matsudaira, who hated Okitsugu's politics. In an effort to improve public morality, Matsudaira initiated the Kansei reforms, so named because of the era in which they fell. Among their many edicts, the reforms banned unsun karuta, and soon the only karuta games that remained were educational ones like iroha-garuta.

It was around this time that the flower-inspired "hana-garuta" was developed. It was the predecessor to that masterpiece of Japanese card games, hanafuda.

The concepts behind hana-garuta were not derived from unsun karuta. Unsun karuta, like Western playing cards, used a combination of suit and number—but it was these numbers that were seen as the source of the cards' menace to public morality, and so they were banned.

In response, card artisans conceived of a way around the restrictions by using the months of the year to stand in for card enumeration, and referring to those months via symbolic pictures on the cards. January would be represented by a crane in a pine tree; October by a stag amid red leaves. The distinction from unsun karuta was further strengthened by the fact that hana-garuta used a 48-card deck comprised of 12 suits, with four cards in each suit, rather than the four-suit, 12 card system of some earlier karuta variations.

The commoners of Edo took to the new gambling cards rapidly, and their popularity soon exploded. However, it was only the latest step in the constant game of cat-and-mouse between the government and the card makers.

The more popular hanafuda became, the more pressure the *bakufu* brought to bear. In 1841, Tadakuni Mizuno instituted the Tenpo Reforms, which among other things banned Edo karuta and hanafuda completely.

Fusajiro Yamauchi would found his card company 48 years later, which coincided perfectly with the next boom in card game popularity.

His timing was uncanny. He had truly inherited both the enterprising spirit of the karuta craftsmen, who constantly changed the "software" of their product in order to survive, and the keen insight necessary to take advantage of the rapidly-changing society.

In 1868, the Edo shogunate fell, ushering in the Meiji restoration, but karuta remained forbidden. Like the shogunate before it, the

Meiji government held gambling to be a vice and prohibited the sale of all non-educational karuta cards—as well as the hanafuda cards commonly used in underground gambling dens.

But the situation changed with the reintroduction of Western-style playing cards that came with the lifting of Japan's isolationist policy. These cards had not been seen since the arrival of Portuguese traders in the 16th century.

The Japanese word for Western playing cards is "toranpu," derived from the English word "trump." The term came about when Japanese saw Westerners playing a variety of bridge, and calling out "trump." "Trump" was mistaken for the name of the game, and soon became an established term for playing cards in Japan—so the story goes.

In any case, Westernization came in a great wave. Intellectuals ate sukiyaki and sweet bean pastries—and they played cards. Though gambling remained illegal, the importation of playing cards was allowed under the pro-Western trade policies of the time. Before long, people were arguing that the ban on the sale of hanafuda and other forms of domestically produced karuta should be lifted.

So it came to pass that in 1885, hanafuda sales were legalized, and in 1889, the ban on other varieties of karuta was lifted as well—and it was that year that Fusajiro opened his shop.

Though Fusajiro was a Meiji-era artisan, in his business acumen in anticipating and taking advantage of the trends of his era, he comes across like a modern venture capitalist.

With the lifting of the ban, hanafuda became explosively popular, perhaps as a backlash to the rapid Westernization of Japan. Sales of the cards rode the wave. Illegal gambling also rose, spurred on by the lifting of the ban.

But history repeats itself. In 1902, a heavy tax was levied on all varieties of karuta in an attempt to improve public morality. The boxer rebellion in China, followed by the beginning of the Russo-Japanese War, spurred on efforts to strengthen the nation's wealth and military power, which required money.

Under the new tax, shop after hanafuda shop folded, and even in Kyoto, the once prosperous industry fell to its knees as increasing numbers of artisans found themselves out of work.

But Nintendo survived.

Fusajiro had the foresight to set his sights on Western-style playing cards, which had previously been available exclusively via import. He used the expertise gained in making hanafuda, and the same year the karuta tax was enacted, he introduced Japan's first domestically produced Western-style playing cards. Furthermore, his exploitation of novel promotional avenues expanded sales from western Japan out to cover the entire nation.

In 1890, Kichibei Murai had succeeded in becoming the first person to manufacture and sell paper-rolled cigarettes within Japan. In a few short years he was known nationwide as the "Tobacco King of the Orient." Fusajiro used Murai's tobacco distribution apparatus to sell his playing cards, massively expanding his business.

Hanafuda and Western playing cards were roughly the size of a pack of cigarettes. The two commodities were also compatible insofar as gamblers tended to use both. Fusajiro, like Murai, operated out of Kyoto, and with Murai's friendship, Fusajiro was able to gain his cooperation.

With competition disappearing, and helped by the use of the cigarette distribution network, Nintendo's sales skyrocketed. By the beginning of the Showa period—1926—Nintendo was the largest card company in Japan.

In 1926, Sekiryo Yamauchi took his place as the second head of the company, renaming it Yamauchi Nintendo, building a new, concrete company headquarters, and improving manufacturing efficiency. At the same time, he established a manufacturing and sales subsidiary called Marufuku, created an independent distribution network, and solidified the company's hanafuda and playing card business.

"Karuta - Playing Cards - Manufacturer - Yamauchi Nintendo"

The historic plaque is still there on the front of the silent old company headquarters in Kyoto, not far from the Kamo river.

400 years have passed since karuta's introduction to Japan; hanafuda goes back 200 years, and it has been 120 years since the founding of

Nintendo. The karuta industry had tasted both the delicious triumph and bitter hardship of the amusement business, developing a software orientation as it adapted to an ever-changing environment. Nintendo, whose roots lie in that industry's greatest achievement, hanafuda, inherited the spirit of the karuta makers of old.

Its founder, Fusajiro, saw through the changing times and adapted to the marketplace in a way no other card maker did. Yamauchi inherited Fusajiro's spirit and led Nintendo onto the world stage. Iwata now tries to carry that spirit on into the future.

Carrying on the spirit—perhaps that has ever been the destiny of Nintendo.

8

Seeds of Fresh Surprise

"We've started talking about how maybe there's no reason to define games so strictly."

—Iwata

Post *Brain-Age* Innovation

It's like when you made little animations in the margins of your grade-school textbooks, and flipped the pages to set them in motion—only now, children aren't using pencils and textbooks or notebooks, but the Nintendo DSi.

They can draw letters or pictures with the stylus, connect them into frames of animation, then add a voice track. What's more, the person they might show these animations to isn't just the kid next to them—it could be someone halfway around the world.

December 2008 saw the release of an unconventional piece of DSi-oriented software. It was called *Flipnote Studio*, and it let users create and share flipbook-style animations, complete with voiceover. *Flipnote Studio* was released on a new game distribution service, "Nintendo DSi Shop," which let users download simple puzzle games and the like, which were generally priced around a few hundred yen. *Flipnote Studio* was one of the pieces of "DSi Ware" available on the service—and it was free.

Animations created on the DSi could be shared via the internet, and users could collaborate with any number of their fellow animators. The resulting content can be viewed not only on the DSi itself, but also on cell phones and PCs, via the website that was established for that express purpose.

Just two short months later, the site had exploded with countless works, and the fans who flocked to view them.

The site is called "Flipnote Hatena," and animations uploaded via the DSi are publicly displayed on the site.

To create this experience, Nintendo turned to Japanese internet service company Hatena, to whom they entrusted the creation and management of the site. Nintendo anticipated a huge amount of content and traffic, so partnering with a company that already had experience in this area was essential.

By early February 2009, just two months after the launch, so many animations had been uploaded—over 240,000 individual works—that it would be hopeless to try to watch them all.

At the time, the animation that consistently topped the site's ranking system was called "Puchi Puchi vs. Boningen" ("Bubble Wrap vs. Stick Figure"). Load it up, and a roughly 30-second animation will play, with a high-pitched chipmunk-like voice providing the character dialog.

"Bubble Wrap vs. Stick Figure! Whoosh! Hey, what's this? All right, bubble wrap! Cool, I'm gonna pop 'em all! Wah-tah!"

The rough, doodle-like drawings play back in rapid succession as the stick figure pops each of the bubble wrap's bubbles, until there's only one left. He flies into the air and comes crashing down, missing the remaining bubble; the impact breaks his arm. Finally, he's hit by a train, goes flying over the horizon, and disappears into a gigantic explosion. The story ends with the caption "Bubble wrap wins."

To be honest, it was hard for your correspondent to understand why this was so popular. But the hundreds of comments people had left were generally along the following lines: "It's hilarious no matter how many times I watch it!" "So funny!" "Can't wait for your next one." The praise rolled on.

"Taakumi," the user who created the animation, is a fourth-grade elementary school student. He's not a brilliant artist, nor was his soundtrack particularly elaborate. But in the world of *Flipnote*, he is a maestro with a large and devoted following.

When you examine the handwritten comments, you see they're shakily written in the phonetic *hiragana* script; it's clear that most of the fans are children. It's impossible not to think back to that fleeting time when all it took was the mention of a word like "bomb" or "explosion" to elicit guffaws. Nintendo and Hatena have created a community where children can apply their own aesthetic standards.

Within two months after the site's opening, Taakumi had already created almost 60 animations, which had been viewed over two million times. Popular creators are born every day, along with tens of thousands of fans. The *Flipnote* boom is stimulating a resurgence of the popularity of the DS.

As mentioned previously, it was in late 2005 that the system's popularity exploded in Japan. The main battleground for the DS has now moved overseas to the US and Europe, and sales have declined in Japan; gone are the days when they were consistently sold out.

As Iwata often says, the domestic sales for 2006—over 9 million units—were "unusual," and there's hardly cause for concern should those numbers fall. From the perspective of per-capita adoption rates, even achieving half of Japan numbers in the 330 million-person marketplace of North America or the 500 million people in Europe is excellent performance.

However, with the rapid acceleration of the Western markets, the difference between sales domestically and abroad is increasing disproportionate to population.

In the second quarter of 2008, for every one DS that was sold in Japan, 4.7 were sold in North America, and 6.3 in Europe (including Asia and other regions). Sales in Japan had fallen to a quarter of what they had been during that same period the previous year.

The problem is saturation. By June of 2008, 23 million units had been sold in Japan. About one in every five people in Japan owns a DS. Have they reached the limit of what can reasonably be sold?

Iwata doesn't think so. There's a plan to give the stagnant Japanese DS market a shot in the arm—and that's the new model designed to be "my DS," unveiled in October 2008: the DSi.

The DSi's selling points are its integrated camera and SD card reader, which allows the unit to play music.

But they're not meant for practical use—the unit's built-in photograph and audio manipulation software are meant to add value by creating new ways to play. The camera makes use of an image sensor with a mere 0.3 megapixels—seasoned technology.

Sales picked up. After its release in the fourth quarter of 2008, domestic DS sales were 1.97 million, on par with the same quarter a year earlier. The DSi comprised 1.66 million of those, contributing

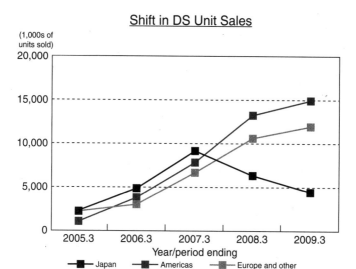

Shift in DS Unit Sales

(1,000s of units sold)

Year/period ending

Japan — Americas — Europe and other

Note: Estimated data for period ending March 2009.

significantly to the platform's revival. The numbers were approaching the ideal Japan–North America–Europe sales ratio of 1:2:2.

Iwata, however, is not satisfied with this. At the same time that domestic hardware sales fell, he was worried by another problem: the marked lack of any new, innovative games to follow up successes like *Brain Age* and *Nintendogs*.

As of April 2009, there were 25 Nintendo DS titles that had sold over 1 million copies. Of those, the biggest seller launched after 2007 is *Pokémon Platinum*, in 7th place, along with only seven other titles. Worse, leave out games in well-known series like *Mario*, *Pokémon*, and *Dragon Quest*—that is to say, games practically guaranteed a certain amount of success—and there is but a single game that remains, a rhythm game called *Rhythm Heaven*, released in August 2008.

Strictly speaking, *Rhythm Heaven* is a sequel itself, to a similarly titled Game Boy Advance title released in August 2006. The innovative "Touch Generations" series of games, which began with *Brain Age*, was steadily dying.

Nintendo is a company whose strengths are expressed in software. If they couldn't create a piece of software that would express the appeal of the DSi the way that *Brain Age* did for the DS, they would be failing to live up to their own company name. To do the DSi justice would require innovation. *Flipnote Studio* was the test.

The result now is that a single child like Taakumi can become a nationwide hero in an instant. This signals the commencement of Iwata's next great strategy.

Bringing Creation to Everyone

"As to why we feel there is such possibility within UGC via the internet is that the fun generated with UGC can be appreciated by a larger fraction of our customers," said Iwata at a financial results briefing in January 2009. "UGC" refers to "user-generated content" or customers' own software output.

There's YouTube, the world's largest video-sharing site, Nico Nico Doga, a Japanese videosharing and captioning site with 10 million users, mixi, Japan's largest social networking site, and of course the countless blogs.

So-called Consumer-Generated Media (CGM) is becoming the internet norm, with sites that rely solely on content created by professionals falling into disuse. Most CGM is created by the same people who once enjoyed professional content. It is the very definition of user-generated content.

Would it be possible to bring the model of UGC to the world of games? Iwata has cast his eye to the problem.

It goes without saying that Nintendo employs first-rate game designers, who will "flip the table" as many times as it takes to polish a game. The company's strict standards also demand quality work from external developers.

Filling games with situations that surprise and delight users—this is the purview of game creators, and this was once enough to keep those users happy. But now, says Iwata, "Our customers are getting used to these stimuli, and they're becoming impossible to surprise. In fact, once they've experienced something, they think, 'Well, I've figured that one out.' Once they've got a game figured, it's easy for them to stop playing it or sell it off. If possible, we'd like to avoid having players think they've gotten a game completely figured out."

Enter UGC. It's impossible to know what kind of content amateurs will produce for a given game—it's like a treasure chest. Such a game would have an inexhaustible longevity.

Hidden within UGC is the possibility for an amateur to create the kind of surprise and delight a professional never could. This is why even as Iwata released the DSi, with its net-based design, he also created software and spaces that would allow users to participate in content creation.

In essence, the DS platform had once been the sole territory of professionals, but now he was declaring the gates open. After increasing the gaming population, the logical next step was to increase the game-*creating* population. *Flipnote Studio* was the first salvo in that campaign.

No sooner had the *Flipnote Studio* website opened on Christmas Eve 2008 than content began to pour in. It took only 16 days for the number of submitted animations to pass 100,000. Works accumulated with terrifying speed, and the rising enthusiasm of fans painted a very clear picture of just how fun and surprising users were finding the experience.

Iwata divides the people who enjoy UGC into two broad categories. To wit, there's "the type who tries to make something creative, and derives pleasure from other people enjoying their work," and "the type who provides the audience for the first type, by applauding their work." In other words, among amateurs there are still creators and players.

The coexistence of these two types is a self-reinforcing cycle; the audience helps draw people into the act of creation, and the new creations help increase the audience.

In the case of *Flipnote Studio*, players looking for interesting works found Taakumi's pieces, liked them, and spread them around. And because the more he created, the more reactions he got, Taakumi threw himself into the process, creating over 60 animations. And for his trouble, he's gotten over 2 million views and 2,000 comments.

In the world of *Flipnote Studio*, popular creators like Taakumi are born every day, bringing with them an ever-increasing audience of players.

Flipnote Studio even allows users to download other creators' works and use them as starting points to create derivative pieces. A user named "Sukai" created a four-panel comic strip with the speech bubbles left deliberately blank. It spawned over 900 variations over the course of two months, as other creators filled in the dialogue and even added new artwork.

Both creators and consumers are users of the software; both are engaging it. *Flipnote Studio* is a new kind of game that can expand autonomously, without intervention from professional creators.

A third category of game is rising, distinct not only from traditional videogames but also from recent innovations like *Brain Age*. Iwata is strategically positioning these new user-centric games to support the DSi.

Naturally, the world of UGC is wildly variant in a way that professional content isn't. Although there are ranking systems that allow the community to self-evaluate, supporting high quality works while allowing less interesting pieces to fall, there is always the risk that children may create works that are inappropriate or in violation of a copyright.

If restrictions are too tight, users will leave, but left alone, problematic content can become a legal liability. Dealing with these issues requires a high degree of expertise, as does creating a system that can handle a high degree of load. That was why Nintendo partnered with internet services company Hatena to create the animation sharing site for *Flipnote Studio*, .

When Iwata heard of the plan to allow users to share animations created in *Flipnote*, he anticipated that it would take them until the second half of 2009 to do it themselves. There was a glut of projects for games and services that used the internet. The schedule stretched on and on.

While the *Flipnote* project was interesting, it was short on staff. Just as Iwata was despairing of how to proceed, the word "Hatena" appeared in his mind.

At around 800,000 registered users, Hatena's scale was not large, but it was a venerable and respected presence in the Japanese internet industry nonetheless. Founder and president Junya Kondo created the company after he graduated from Kyoto University in 2001, and Mochio Umeda, well-known technology consultant and author of *Webu Shinkaron* ("On Web Evolution") serves on its board of directors. Iwata had met Umeda many times, and began to wonder if they could do something together.

Even better, Hatena's headquarters were also in Kyoto. If they collaborated, the *Flipnote* schedule would move forward much more quickly, and it would be an educational experience for Nintendo to boot. Iwata wasted no time in contacting Hatena.

In December 2008 at a press conference at Hatena's headquarters, *Flipnote Studio*'s producer, Nintendo EAD's Yoshiaki Koizumi, said this: "I think gameplay like this, that can expand by using a built-in editor, is a very important direction for Nintendo. I also think the things we learned by being able to work with Hatena are really important for that direction."

Hatena designed the site with a filtering system that let users report inappropriate content—the user base is self-policing. Although submitted animations are automatically published on the Flipnote Hatena site, they don't appear on the DSi-exclusive Flipnote Theater site until a set period of time has passed. If during that time even one user marks the animation as inappropriate, it is suspended until the site staff can check it and decide whether or not to publish the submission.

Two months after the site went live, there had been no major problems with Hatena's management, and the self-policing system was working well.

However, a handful of issues came up, including disputes involving users—how to decide when a child had taken their joke too

187

far, whether to approve the use of a preexisting character like Mario in someone's animation, whether or not copyrighted music capture via the DSi's microphone was subject to copyright fees…

Yet problems like these are inevitable whenever a new culture of play is invented, and solving them would yield the experience necessary to power further innovation. Nintendo has placed itself at the front lines of that innovation.

And Iwata is "excited," he says.

In the issue of the "The President Asks" series on Nintendo's website that coincided with the DSi's launch, Iwata wrote:

> I'm kind of excited, myself. The world of videogames has been mostly closed, but now it's being connected to the mostly open world of the internet. I wonder how people are going to use it?

He also says:

> Now you can take whatever you create with this and share it with the whole world. Now anyone with talent, no matter how remote or hidden they might be, has the chance to have their work seen by anyone, anywhere.

Within that work, some of it is on par with professional-level content, and some of it is unlike anything a game company would imagine. Iwata is filled with anticipation at what these creators may bring to the world of the DS.

What he's looking forward to is much more than flipbook cartoons. Game creation itself is a possibility. And in fact, in 2009, Nintendo plans to release software for the DS that does exactly that.

In autumn 2008, Nintendo announced a game that would allow anyone to create and share simple microgames of their own devising. It was called *WarioWare D.I.Y.*

It's the only game in the world that lets players choose backgrounds and characters, create music, and set up rules. Details are scant, but Nintendo plans to include network awareness such that players can collaborate. The resulting games will be playable not only on the DS, but also the Wii.

It is an experiment, to try to turn people who were once passive players of games into true creators. Signs that it may well be a success are already showing up.

Hatena keeps track of hot topics on the Flipnote Hatena site, and every week it distributes the "Flipnote Hatena News." In the issue for February 13, 2009, which included the following feature: "Mazes, quizzes, and slot machines! You guys are great! A special report on some special Flipnotes!"

For example, one animation had a cup being rapidly filled with water. The goal is to hit the pause button just in time for the water to fill the brim. "Game-like" pieces are increasing on the service; although the graphics don't respond to controls, players have created quizzes and mazes, and there are even some series of animations that tell a story based on viewer's choices, just like the choose-your-own-adventure books you might have read as a kid.

The DSi was released in the Americas in April 2009, and shortly thereafter in Europe. It was the first step in the exportation of Nintendo's strategy of increasing the number of people who don't just play games, but create them.

For animation and microgames, the language barrier is relatively low. Now people from anywhere in the world can create and share delight and surprise that no professional designer could possibly imagine.

Where a professional might be at a loss, some amateur could change the world. The DSi holds that potential.

The Restoration of the Living Room

In January 2009, the day after Nintendo announced a downward adjustment of its financial forecast, the company's stock nosedived to 28,300 yen, just a bit over half its level a year earlier.

Despite the downward adjustment, they still broke their own

records for earnings and operating profit—but nonetheless, given that Nintendo had exceeded its own projections every quarter since April 2006, the downward adjustment was enough to inspire concern in shareholders.

Meanwhile, the rest of the world was mired in a recession, and starting around the middle of 2008, the persistence of industry rumors like "Nintendo's peaked already" or "their performance is gonna drop starting March 2009" depressed the stock price.

The DS had just passed its fourth year, and the market wanted to hear news of a new model. But Nintendo seemed entirely disinclined to move to another hardware generation—far from it, with their new program to create internet-enabled software for the DS, they seemed to be ready to set off a two-stage rocket.

The story was the same with the Wii.

"In Spring 2009, we will introduce the *Wii no Ma* channel, a video service that will let you use your Wii to take back the living room." So went the December 2008 press release—only one page long, but bearing a critical message. The companies involved were Nintendo and one other—Dentsu, Japan's largest advertising agency.

Wii no Ma ("Wii Living Room") aimed to reproduce the family living room, where members gather to enjoy television. A family's Miis would all gather in the Wii no Ma to tune into various events.

What kind of events? Video content. But this wasn't just a video content delivery system—Nintendo was delivering family-oriented video content packaged as a game, and their plans for the system were not limited to Japan.

Dentsu acted as an intermediary between Nintendo and the broadcasters and production companies—*Wii no Ma* would not distribute programs from their archives, but rather new content produced expressly for the channel.

The details of what types of programming would be available will not be clear until the channel's launch in spring 2009, but the simple fact that Dentsu is getting involved with a game machine ensures that the system will have significant impact.

In 2008, the large media players fell into an unprecedented recession in advertising.

According to Dentsu's report on advertising spending in Japan for 2008, total nationwide advertising outlays fell 4.7% to 6.6926 trillion yen. It was the first drop in five years.

Although internet advertising rose 16.3% to 698.3 billion, coming in a solid third behind television and newspapers, the "four media" of television, newspapers, magazines, and radio have, taken in sum, sustained losses for four straight years. It's the first time the four media's share of ad money has fallen below 50% since statistics started being collected in 1947, and it emphasized both the rise of internet advertising and the decline of traditional media.

Thus Dentsu is desperate to grab onto any change in the circumstances that have beset advertising. At the end of 2008, some 45 million Wii units had been sold, 80% of which were installed in living rooms, and 40 percent of which were internet-connected. The male/female distribution of users is about 50-50 and encompasses a wide age range.

Which means that over 18 million Wiis worldwide and 3.1 million in Japan connect their living rooms to the internet, and can take on the same duties as the TV programming in those same living rooms. It makes for an attractive ad medium, given the unique advertising possibilities opened up by the Wii.

Can the the Wii, as a videogame system, really become a platform for video? *Minna no Theater Wii* ("Everybody's Wii Theater"), a video-on-demand service, is the first indication that it can.

The service began in January 2009. It lets users order from an archive of around 3,000 vintage cartoons, superhero shows, documentaries, and more, streaming DVD-quality video for titles like *Astro Boy*, *Yatterman*, *Kamen Rider*, and *Project X*.

It seems like it would be one of the channels on the Wii Menu, but it's not. Instead, it's one of the pieces of software sold through WiiWare, a system for selling small, moderately priced (between 500 and 1,000 yen) games for the Wii. It was created by Fujisoft, a major software company, and is not managed my Nintendo.

One possible reason it's not found among the Wii Menu channel selections is that its contents are limited to video, plain and simple—it has none of the game-like flourishes that characterize Wii Menu channels. Still, four weeks after the opening of the service, it was the most-downloaded item among the roughly 80 available WiiWare titles.

Net-enabled television services are proliferating; examples include acTVila, from a consortium of flat-panel TV manufacturers, and NTT's Hikari-TV IPTV service, but *Minna no Theater Wii* is unique among them in its use of the Wii as a video playback device.

There is a very real possibility that between its Nintendo-like sense of fun and the power of Dentsu's content, the Wii no Ma channel will exceed *Minna no Theater Wii* in popularity.

In the spring of 2009, Japanese food delivery portal Demae-can, an internet service connected to 8,500 restaurants and which handles over 500,000 orders every month, will bring its service to the Wii. In 2008, karaoke distribution giant XING teamed up with game developer Hudson to introduce *Karaoke JOYSOUND Wii*. The game itself came on a disc, but when connected to the internet offered downloads of over 30,000 songs, with 1,000 new songs added every month.

If lifestyle services like these continue to expand, it seems likely that Iwata may well reach his goal of having the Wii be the first thing users turn on after the TV—and domination of the TV portal market may well be possible.

Before the release of the Wii, when Iwata connected the concepts of "something that you'd turn on right after turning on the TV, something expandable, something network-connected," in his mind, he had said something like this to Takeda, who was working on hardware integration: "Takeda—this could change the relationship between families and TV, games, and the internet."

Nintendo is not involved with simple video distribution. However, they will create a video platform with game-like elements, and leave things like standard video and karaoke to other companies. The same goes for other services developed for the internet.

Essentially, so long as it's more fun than practical—so long as it's not the enemy of videogaming—any service, any content can be be served on the Wii. Says Iwata, "We've started talking about how maybe there's no reason to define games so strictly—that our job is simply to create things that respond in fun ways to human input."

By that logic, having built software around the idea of fitness and weight tracking, building a channel around the idea of video is certainly possible. By collecting and presenting content from the web, the Wii becomes no mere videogame machine, but a multi-function device certainly worthy of the term "set-top box."

When the idea is suggested to Iwata, he has this to say. "It was never my intention to aim for domination of the living room and make a killing in the process, with the Wii. It wasn't that, it was more along the lines of, if we make a box that everyone will like, then it might just naturally take over the living room. Living room domination isn't the goal, but in kind of a guerilla style we seem to have come to a place where we're closest to that goal anyway."

The Assassin from the Sandlot

No one short of the makers themselves has a clear sense of how many makers are creating how many games, and which games are sold in which amounts in which countries. But it is clear enough that the number of games and players alike on this new platform are rising with dizzying speed. The company that created this platform is Apple. The platform itself is the iPhone multifunction smartphone, and its cousin, the iPod Touch, identical save for the lack of a cell phone.

By the end of 2008, the platform had reached one third of the DS's total sales—30 million units. Each one of these devices has access to over ten thousand games.

The portable gaming wars have entered a new phase.

In July 2008, Apple opened its App Store download service for the iPhone and iPod Touch. A sea change had begun.

Weather, electronic books, education, news, navigation… software of every kind proliferated within the App Store.

In March of 2009, the combined number of both free and paid apps was 25,000, and since each of them could be downloaded to the iPhone the same way music could, regardless of time or location, the adoption rate was incredible.

A mere eight months after the App Store opened, it had served in excess of 800 million downloads. And games were helping drive that popularity.

In a flash, it was no exaggeration to call the iPhone and iPod Touch portable game systems.

Of the 20 categories on the App Store, "Games" is the biggest. In March 2009, the number of games available passed ten thousand, far in excess of the 1,300 titles available for the DS at that time. And because the types of games available are not so very different from the DS, this is not something Nintendo can ignore.

What Nintendo was aiming for with the DS was a casual gaming experience, something that would easily fill up small bits of free time here and there. The touch screen made control intuitive and approachable for new players, and game themes ran the gamut from education to music.

…Just like the games collected in the App Store.

Just as the DS and Wii had introduced new interface types, creating un-game-like games that surprised and delighted the world, Apple's new control methods and the games that utilized them were a delight to use.

The iPhone and iPod Touch use a multitouch display; all controls are managed with a touch of the user's finger, from inputting characters to clicking, scrolling, and zooming.

The display's resolution is greater than the DS's, and animation on the display is smooth, fast, and beautiful. And with the addition of gestures to the interface vocabulary, the controls are even more intuitive. The two models are also equipped with accelerometers, allowing them to sense orientation and movement.

The music game *Tap Tap Revenge* is representative.

With simple gameplay that involves tapping the screen and tilting the unit along with various popular songs, just two weeks after its release in July 2008, it was downloaded a million times. By January 2009 it had passed 5 million downloads, and still tops the download rankings for every country it's available in.

In addition to intuitive, innovative games like this, board games like Othello and Mahjong are also available, as well as sports games like tennis, baseball, and auto racing, in addition to a variety of more traditional videogames, all sorted into categories and ranked by number of downloads.

Still more intriguing are the pieces of software that are not games, but that users are finding game-like ways of enjoying.

One such example is a title that has consistently been in the top ten downloads for Japan—publisher Sanseido's *Daijirin* dictionary. Users can leave comments and reviews for any app in the App Store. Here are some selections from user comments regarding *Daijirin*.

"It's like you're swimming in an ocean of words. If I hadn't tried it, I would never have guessed it would be this fun. I think it's because it's on the iPhone and iPod Touch that it really feels like a dictionary you can play with."

"It's just a dictionary app, but it's so much fun to use. You'll want to look up words for hours."

"As you go from one word to another, to another, the fun of reading and the fun of knowing just piles up."

As you flip through the index, countless words scroll smoothly by. Enter the definition page for a word, and all you have to do is touch another word within that definition to jump to *its* definition. All the animation is pleasant and smooth. It's just a dictionary—but somehow, on the iPhone's screen, it becomes fun.

Apple's software library and user base are increasing fast enough that they're threatening to steal Nintendo's thunder. And the surprise for Nintendo doesn't end there.

In a twist of irony, Apple's already thoroughly beaten Nintendo to the strategy that Iwata intends to pursue next—that of increasing the number of game creators.

As discussed previously, Iwata's strategy for the future is predicated on user-generated content. The DSi's *Flipnote Studio* as well as the upcoming *WarioWare D.I.Y.* microgame creation kit are the opening salvos in that battle.

However, these only free the user to create content within a particular piece of software. Users aren't free to create and sell software directly for the DS. Ever since the days of the NES, Nintendo has never wavered from its traditional method of strict software control; they maintain a stranglehold on software circulation, carefully evaluating both developers and the games they produce.

Apple's system, by contrast, is the antithesis of Nintendo's. The product manager for the iPod in Japan, Yoshio Ichii, has this to say: "Anyone with a Mac and iPhone to develop on, along with a developers' subscription that costs 10,800 yen per year, can develop an iPhone app and release it worldwide."

In the world of the App Store, there is no distinction between the professional and the amateur. Before being released to the store, an app must pass Apple's inspection, but so long as it's not especially poorly made, and contains no objectionable content, it will pass. In fact, in February 2009, 96% of all apps submitted were made available on the store.

Obviously, the App Store is a mixed bag. There are many titles that are immediately reviewed as "crappy games" and summarily dismissed by users.

It's like a game of amateur sandlot baseball—there's no shame in striking out, so people keep stepping up to the plate. But developing for Nintendo or Sony, that's the major leagues—and they'll only send up batters that won't embarrass them.

But in a marketplace with a potential audience of 30 million, individuals and tiny venture-funded startups can dream big. Bad games will get beaten down, but great games will find an audience. In a competitive marketplace, novel, interesting games will be born every day.

Another aspect of the App Store culture that contributes to the potential success of a game is that of the free promotional version.

Many games offer free versions, with the field of play or features restricted. Allowing users to try a game before they buy the full version, amplified by the effect of word-of-mouth, can lead to sales of the paid version of the game.

What's more, most of those games are between 105 and 500 yen; only a few approach 1,000 yen. That may seem small, but if you sell 100,000 copies of a 105 yen game, that's 10.5 million yen. Apple takes 30% of App Store sales, which leaves the developer 7.35 million yen. That's peanuts to a giant game developer, but to an individual or small company, it's real money. And so they work feverishly to create new, innovative games.

It took a team of just four people to create *Tap Tap Revenge*, the free version of which was downloaded 5 million times. Of those, over 100,000 bought the paid version. The software company responsible, Tapulous, has gone on to create another revenue stream via promotions with record companies.

Employed at a software company but working alone, a single Japanese engineer created *Pocket Guitar*, an app that realistically simulates guitar playing. Created in his free time, the app went on to be purchased over 500,000 times, yielding at least 35 million yen in profit.

App Store dreams like this one bring the quality up every day. It may be sandlot baseball, but the major leagues can't ignore it forever.

Beginning in late 2008, major game studios like Square Enix, Konami, and Electronic Arts were entering the fray—now professionals, semi-professionals, and amateurs are all fighting it out in the same ring.

Thanks to the App Store, the barriers to entry are now lower than ever, making competition that much fiercer as creators dig for new ideas. Nintendo, too, has started offering inexpensive (between 200 and 800 yen) downloads for the DSi, but development is closed to all but professionals. It's still the major leagues.

Should they open the platform to amateur developers? You can be sure Iwata will be watching Apple's movements very, very closely.

Regarded objectively, Nintendo is in a very comfortable position.

They've enjoyed the success of the DS and the Wii both in Japan and abroad. The scope of their business has expanded from Mario to fitness, and their every venture seems to only bring them more favor. Moving forward, both the DS and the Wii hold within them significant potential for new internet-enabled games and services.

But Iwata himself knows full well that Nintendo cannot afford to indulge in complacency. Even while they're at the top, they must continue to embrace a sense of urgency, for hell is just a stumble away. The reality is that an avalanche of issues is rushing toward them.

Iwata has to be uneasy about what the rise of the iPhone as a game platform could mean for DS software sales. Certainly if the overseas markets are any indication, the million-sellers of old are a dying breed, and the number of people walking around with their DS is also dropping. There's also a limit to how much the overseas holiday season can be relied upon.

Just as Iwata himself said at a financial results meeting in January 2009, "Japan probably has the least vigorous home console market in the world, right now," and while the Wii is still selling well abroad, its declining performance in Japan cannot be denied. In the last quarter of 2008, the Wii sold 9.5 million units in the Americas and Europe, while in Japan sales were a mere 880,000 units.

Since *Wii Fit*, there hasn't been a software title that expanded the platform's territory. *Wii Music*, which was released in Japan in the autumn of 2008, had not yet sold 400,000 copies by March 2009, betraying the expectations of executives.

Nintendo is not faltering, nor is it succumbing to competitors. The simple fact is that upon their release, the DS and Wii surprised everyone, and now there seems to be evidence that that surprise is fading—evidence to support the idea that the adults whose attention was captured by the Wii are now becoming bored.

But again, Iwata understands that better than anyone.

When asked at a financial results meeting what he thought about the rumor that Apple might be seriously looking to enter the game market, he said, "Rather than talking about risks like that, I think it's much more important to figure out how to put out the next big thing before our customers get bored with what's currently supporting us. If we can do that, then we'll continue to be supported, and if we can't, then very soon people will start claiming that we've peaked—so I'd like to do it properly."

Sony and Microsoft, and even Apple—these are not Nintendo's enemies. No, Iwata is well aware that the company's true enemy is boredom. Whatever surprise you create today becomes your enemy tomorrow.

And the plan to address this is already in motion.

Five Christmases have passed since the release of the DS, and there hasn't been so much as a whisper about a new hardware platform. Both the media and people involved with the marketplace are assuming that Nintendo is postponing news about the next hardware generation for the foreseeable future. Analyst Masashi Morita of Okasan Securities makes this prediction: "I don't expect new hardware from Nintendo until around 2013. Until then, expect minor changes to the DS and Wii. We've seen them go from the DS to the DS Lite, to the DSi, so next will be the 'DS something-or-other.' Sony and Microsoft, too, are going to be taking action to repair their current business before they think about the next hardware generation."

But DS and Wii software and services that are designed for surprise will continue.

Yoichi Wada, president of Square Enix, says: "I think that the gameplay gimmicks that things like the touch screen and accelerometer made possible are mostly exhausted. The next challenge for Nintendo is probably going to be how many ideas they can pull from the networking angle."

Naturally, Nintendo is a self-acknowledged software-oriented company, and they surely have plans in effect to hammer out a couple more hits. The chances of new announcements for June 2009's E3 conference are good.

At a financial results briefing in January 2009, Iwata commented, looking ahead to E3: "We're always trying all kinds of things. We move from one presentation to the next, and sometimes it's received the way we'd like it to be, and sometimes the reception isn't as good. But in the end, the one who controls the videogame market is the one who can successfully create that single explosively popular product."

Iwata indicates that for the DS, that "explosively popular product" was *Brain Age* and *Nintendogs*; for the Wii it was *Wii Sports* and *Wii Fit*. "It terrifies me to think what might have happened had we not created those products," says Iwata. "It's that kind of hit software that gets customer after customer to buy the hardware just to play it. And then they invite their friends, and it spreads from there. That's why we had the DS phenomenon and the Wii phenomenon. We've got to keep trying to create those kind of experiences. Of course, we'll be bringing out new proposals this year, and working hard to live up to people's expectations."

Iwata is still aiming for home runs on both the DS and Wii that will have the impact of *Brain Age* and *Wii Fit*. But it would be rash to neglect research into the hardware that will deliver the next generation of surprises.

"In the world of amusement, once you see that new, epochal thing, it makes whatever you've been playing with up to that point look inevitably old. So we have to keep doing hardware research. Once we release a piece of hardware, we start on the next one immediately. But the release timing isn't something that we decide—it's when all the circumstances align that we can say 'oh, now's the time' and see when the release will actually be."

Just as Iwata suggests, he is in all likelihood already dealing with several hardware prototypes. Or perhaps Miyamoto and his team are hard at work on new controller concepts.

The tireless research into new surprises continues. A certain investment made by Iwata is proof of his resolve.

In February 2009, a 12.8 billion yen investment came to light. And yet it was not the acquisition of a software company. Nintendo had bought the driving range that was located less than 200 meters from its headquarters, a site totaling roughly 40,000 square meters.

Indeed, it was the very same driving range where Miyamoto had been struck with the idea of putting a touch screen on the DS while talking with Iwata. The property had been purchased as part of a plan to construct a new research facility.

Nintendo moved to its current facility in 2000. Its previous quarters were dubbed "Kyoto Research Park," and one of the R&D sections was left there. The once-divided R&D sections will be integrated at the new site, enabling hardware and software projects to progress in a more unified fashion.

It's impossible not to be excited at the news that development on the post-DS, post-*Brain Age*, post-Wii and -*Wii Fit* era is even now being single-mindedly pursued. After all, just across the way, the very heart of delight and surprise is becoming more concrete every day.

Says Iwata: "If I said we had ideas stretching ten years ahead, I'd be lying. But as an organization, we've gotten very good at creating the circumstances that will lead to those ideas."

Nintendo has inherited the endurance and ingenuity of a long-lived karuta maker. They've overcome countless difficulties in order to survive in the amusement business. They've learned strategies like software orientation and lateral thinking with seasoned technology in order to create hits, becoming strong in the way that only the brutal toy industry requires.

In an era when change and reform are *de rigueur*, this group of proud craftsmen has not wavered from their dedication to the creation of fun. Yet, they can boast of their innovation along that path, as their revolutionaries have delivered surprise and delight to the world—and they continue to meet those challenges.

In the constantly shifting world of amusement, things do not always go as one would wish. They know the value of good fortune and the limits of effort, and leaving luck to heaven, they toil away heroically, unconcerned with the pressure they face.

It is truly the era of software. It's an era saturated with more *things* than we need.

The age of basic functionality, of durability, has passed. Consumers' eyes have been captured by design, by user experience, and by convenience.

Most every piece of hardware in the world has a computer of some kind in it, and it's not the hardware itself but the quality of the software that harnesses it that differentiates a product.

When it comes to home electronics, a company can—without releasing a new product—release an update to a product's software via the network, and almost magically turn the same product into something entirely new for the customer.

But in what way should the hardware be changed? How should it be used? And how will that work out for the bottom line? It's no exaggeration to suggest that these decisions can determine the fate of a company.

Manufacturing has long been revered in the hardware-focused Japanese economy. Nintendo is rare in that while it does create hardware, it understands the primacy of software. It took time for that potential to come to obvious fruition in the world marketplace. But that time has certainly arrived.

Will they once again be able to overcome their own limitations to bring smiles to the faces of consumers? Nintendo's singular formula for success is once again being tested.

The hero of Nintendo's revival, Yamauchi, grins as he finishes off his own interview in memorable style. "When you're all out of ideas and you don't know what to do, you gotta fold the company. If we get stuck in such a place, well, what to do? There's nothing to be done. Turn into a hardware company? Can't be done."

When you can't bring your talents to bear—if you're going to lose the one thing you've got to protect—it's better to close up shop. When

203

its sword is bent and it's all out of arrows, Nintendo will simply end.

With that steely resolve in its heart, the company continues to apply new seeds into its formula and to search for solutions.

* * *

Update—For the English Edition
Nine months have passed since the publication of the Japanese edition of *Nintendo Magic*. It is now February 2010. In that time, there have been two important events, each of which give important clues regarding Nintendo's direction. With this epilogue, I would therefore like to bring the English edition up to date with some facts.

The first important event came in June 2009, at E3, a conference any company involved with the videogame industry cannot afford to ignore.

In the original epilogue to this book, I wrote: "Naturally, as a self-acknowledged software-oriented company, Nintendo surely has plans in effect to hammer out a couple more hits. The chances of new announcements for June 2009's E3 conference are good."

As expected, at the end of their press conference, Nintendo gave us a glimpse of their new idea, straight from Satoru Iwata's mouth. It was the Wii Vitality Sensor, a device capable of sending vital information like heart rate ("and more") to the Wii.

Like always, Iwata spoke extensively on the success of Nintendo's push to broaden the appeal of videogames as he began to introduce the new games that would pick up where *Brain Age* and *Wii Fit* left off.

The words "Wii Vitality Sensor" were displayed on the large projector screen behind him as Iwata stood on the black stage, clad in a black suit. In his right hand he held a Wii Remote, but capping his left index finger and connected to the remote was a device of unfamiliar design.

"Just as we're able to sense the player's center of balance in *Wii Fit*, we're now able to sense their body's internal state. Where previous games have only been sources of excitement and stimulation, now we'll be able to relieve stress and encourage better sleep," he told a stunned audience.

The new peripheral fits over the player's index finger and measures their heart rate. A horror game can now sense whether a player is actually scared—or a yoga game can measure a player's relaxation level. Games that use the new device are due out in the middle of 2010.

Similar fragments of information were disseminated at the media briefing, but there was no further information given. As of January 2010, no more details had been announced, but this is already enough information to give us a sense of the new surprises Nintendo is preparing to follow up the North American-centric success of the Wii Balance Board and *Wii Fit*. It goes without saying that those surprises will not be limited to a simple heart-rate monitor.

What follows is speculation, but it seems likely that at the June 2010 E3, Nintendo will outline its plan for *Wii Relax*, which will be packaged with the Wii Vitality Sensor and released in time for the 2010 holiday season. At a financial results briefing in July 2009, Iwata declared: "We'd like to first bring out a game based around the idea of relaxation, sometime in mid-2010," and by the beginning of 2010 Nintendo had registered "Wii Relax" as a trademark in both Europe and the United States—their direction is clear.

This new class of software promises to discern a user's "autonomic balance" from their pulse, inferring their stress level and degree of relaxation. As it collects this data over time, it will draw a clear picture of the user's mental state. As the name suggests, it will no doubt include games of some kind to help lead the user to a state of relaxation. Having addressed the brain and body, Nintendo is now taking aim at the mind.

Brain Age, an explosive breakout hit for the DS, and *Wii Fit*, the game that gave the Wii incredible traction even in the midst of a terrible recession, are both examples of a new kind of videogame, a class of software that transcends old definitions and is directly concerned with the player's health. By applying this principle to the concept of a game designed to improve a player's mental state, it is reasonable to imagine that this, too, will be another key piece in the ongoing effort to grow the gaming population.

With the release of *Wii Music* in the fall of 2008, and its subsequent failure to reach the same heights as *Brain Age* and *Wii Fit*, the voices in the videogame industry wondering aloud if the Wii was losing its appeal have grown louder. But Nintendo is constantly working to create new surprises—to exceed the bar they themselves have set with their previous efforts. And at E3 2009, they gave a glimpse of a part of those efforts.

In October 2009, at the mid-year fiscal results and corporate strategy briefing, Iwata said this: "I believe that many of our customers, when they start recording their weight every day using Wii Fit, come to understand the effects their activities have on their weight. I myself have discovered that when I eat out, it goes straight to my gut. And now, with the upcoming Wii Vitality Sensor, we think we'll be able to help people understand things about their health that a simple weight check could never show. If I talk about it too much it will spoil the surprise, so I hope you'll understand when I say only that it is much more than a simple device for measuring heart rate."

It is impossible not to feel some anticipation at the confidence implied by Iwata's statement. At the very least, it is clear that suggesting Nintendo's cycle of innovation has stopped is premature.

But at the results and strategy meeting that was the source for this comment, it was unavoidable that there also be some more bearish statements—just a day earlier, the first-quarter revenue forecast had been adjusted significantly downward.

As discussed in the prologue, Nintendo powered unaffected through the 2008 holiday season, a season which otherwise trembled from the impact of the credit crisis that the "Lehman Shock" of September 2008 precipitated. As a result, their sales for the fiscal year ending March 2009 were up 9.9% from the previous year, to 1.8386 trillion yen, with operating profit up 14% to 555.2 billion yen—a record for the company.

The forecast for the year ending March 2010 was unsurprisingly conservative, but nonetheless amounted to sales of 1.8 trillion yen and operating profit of 490 billion yen, roughly on par with the previous year. Given the difficult environment created by a suffering global economy and mounting exchange rate losses, Nintendo's anticipation of similar results to the previous year without any plan to launch next-generation hardware was a bold statement.

However, upon entering the new fiscal year, the situation worsened. The day after the midyear results briefing (which covered the period from March to September 2009), newspapers ran headlines like "The First Drop in Sales in Four Years—The Wii Boom is Busted."

Sales in the first half of the fiscal year were down 34.5% from the previous year, to 548 billion yen, with operating profit down 58.6% to 104.3 billion yen—the first drop in midyear performance in four years. The main cause was the stalling of the Wii. At 5.75 million units, Wii console sales were down 43% from the same period a year earlier.

"Attitudes toward videogames have cooled more than we expected them to. By this spring, we were expecting that to happen, but to be honest, come summer we realized that we hadn't anticipated the extent to which it would be so. That was our misjudgment," Iwata candidly admitted at the semiannual corporate policy and financial results briefing in October 2009.

In September 2009, Sony dropped the price of the PS3, and for the first time, US sales of the console surpassed those of the Wii. Although Iwata claimed that "sales that result from a price drop have no longevity," Nintendo was forced to follow suit. In late September they dropped the price of the Wii in North America $50 to $199.99, with similar drops in Europe and Japan coming shortly after.

The sagging sales, exacerbated by the price drop, contributed to Nintendo revising their year-end performance estimates downward at the midyear results briefing.

Estimated sales for the fiscal year ending March 2010 dropped 300 billion yen to 1.5 trillion yen, with operating profit likewise dropping to 370 billion yen, down 120 billion yen from the previous estimate.

Net profit was adjusted down 70 billion yen to 230 billion. Compared with the previous year, sales were down 18%, with operating profit plunging 33%—hardly performance on par with 2008.

Had Nintendo finally peaked? Were they approaching the beginning of their decline?

Despair spread throughout the marketplace. By December, the stock price had plunged to 25,000 yen, down 15% since the midyear briefing, and down 42% since the beginning of 2009.

However, even as Iwata was quick to acknowledge "error," it was in no way an admission of "defeat." Was it a temporary setback, or the beginning of a decline? While the marketplace clearly viewed it as the latter, Iwata did not agree.

At the strategy and results briefing, he was very clear about ascribing the Wii's slump to "a shortage of strong game titles."

"The games we sold at the end of 2008 did not display much longevity, and we were unable to launch strong titles in the first half of 2009, so there's been a significant decline in software sales. [...] In order to bring Wii sales back up, this year's titles will be much stronger."

By "this year's titles," Iwata referred to three big releases: *Wii Sports Resort*, which was available worldwide by July 2009, *Wii Fit Plus*, out by October, and *New Super Mario Bros. Wii*, which came out in December.

Iwata's firm posture seemed to say "look at the results for the whole year," a tone echoed by the downward-adjusted performance forecasts. While sales and operating profit estimates for the first half of the 2009 fiscal year were down 35% and 59% respectively, those figures changed to 18% and 33% for the year overall. Unit sales estimates were similar.

For the first half of 2009, the number of units shipped was down 43% to 5.75 million for the hard-hit Wii, but the revised sales estimate for the full year was only down 23% from 2008, at 20 million units. To achieve this figure, the Wii would have to experience second-half sales roughly on par with its previous year. In other words, Nintendo was declaring "The Wii will regain its energy by this holiday season."

So what was the outcome of the 2009 holiday season? This is the other important point we must understand in order to predict Nintendo's future.

Surprisingly, Nintendo succeeded in putting out a number of significant titles. In a global economy still mired in uncertainty, they posted their best figures yet, particularly in the United States—the single biggest videogame market in the world.

When the NPD Group, a US market research firm, published the December 2009 sales results in late January 2010, a shock ran through the world.

The best-selling home console in the United States was the Wii, at 3.81 million units sold over the month—a record for single-month sales of *any* kind of console, portable or home, in that country. The influence of the price drop, as well as the three significant titles released in the bottom half of the year, is clear.

Of the top 10 games for December 2009, six were for a Nintendo platform, and five were Wii games. *New Super Mario Bros. Wii* stood atop the pile, followed by the two other big releases for the Wii.

By the end of that December, just a month and a half after it went on sale, *New Super Mario Bros. Wii* had proven wildly popular, selling 10.55 million copies worldwide. *Wii Sports Resort* had likewise sold 13.58 million copies by that point, with *Wii Fit Plus* moving 10.16 million copies—proof that the Wii platform was clearly still healthy.

Aided by these titles, the cumulative software sales for the Wii rose to 178.04 million, surpassing the previous software sales leader for the current generation of home game consoles, Microsoft's Xbox 360—a platform that had launched a year ahead of the Wii.

Likewise, the DS performed surprisingly well in its sixth holiday season, establishing new records even as it entered old age by the reckoning of the traditional five-year cycle of game platform lifespan. The DSi, a minor update to the DS that included a small camera, was the second best-selling game console in the US in December. The portable system sold 3.31 million units in December 2009, setting a

December 2009 Sales Ranking for U.S. Game Market				
	RANK	PRODUCT	COMPANY	THOUSANDS OF UNITS SOLD
Hardware	1	Wii	Nintendo	3,810
	2	Nintendo DS	Nintendo	3,310
	3	Playstation 3	SCE	1,360
	4	Xbox 360	Microsoft	1,310
	5	PSP	SCE	654.7
	6	PlayStation 2	SCE	333.2
Software	1	New Super Mario Bros. Wii	Wii	2,820
	2	Wii Fit Plus	Wii	2,410
	3	Wii Sports Resort	Wii	1,790
	4	Call of Duty: Modern Warfare 2	Xbox 360	1,630
	5	Call of Duty: Modern Warfare 2	PS3	1,120
	6	Wii Play	Wii	1,010
	7	Mario Kart Wii	Wii	993.6
	8	Assassin's Creed II	Xbox 360	783.1
	9	Left 4 Dead 2	Xbox 360	728.5
	10	Mario & Luigi: Bowser's Inside Story	DS	656.7

new record for monthly sales—sales of a system that had been unveiled in December 2004.

Furthermore, total US sales of the DS in 2009 reached 11.22 million units, a new record for the system. The previous record-holder for most consoles sold in a single year was the Wii in 2008 with 10.23 million units, but Nintendo broke its own record with the DS.

The slump in the Wii's sales had been worse in Japan and Europe, and while performance wasn't record-breaking, Nintendo's business clearly recovered. Satisfied with what had been their best holiday season ever, at the beginning of 2010 Iwata hosted a rare spate of individual interviews with journalists from countless newspapers and wire services, in which he talked up Nintendo's recovery. For example, in an interview with Reuters, he said:

"The Wii has recovered from its slowdown in Japan, Europe, and the US. Several factors contributed to its great worldwide sales. In

Japan, Wii sales for December were the best since 2006. They were so good we missed some opportunities because retailers sold out of the console.

"At the very least, one thing has changed. Compared with January 2009, our momentum in Japan in 2010 is totally different. It's far stronger now. Once you've built up that momentum, the people that played your games talk to other people, and those other people become interested in your product, and the cycle goes on. That's how the DS and Wii grew."

And on January 29, at the third-quarter financial results briefing for the fiscal year ending March 2010, Iwata was able to proclaim, "Nintendo's greatest home console success was the NES, which sold 61.91 million units over its lifetime—but Wii sales just reached 67.45 million units, making it the most successful home console Nintendo has ever made.

"For portable systems, in December 2009, just as the Wii was setting a new record, the DS reached 125.13 million units sold, passing the 118.69 million units sold by the Game Boy series to become the best-selling hardware ever made by Nintendo."

It was still not enough to fully compensate for the slump that preceded it, but the strong results of the holiday season helped turn the balance sheets around. Midway through the fiscal year (the period from April through September 2009), sales were down 35% compared with the previous year's performance, but by the end of December that figure was only 23%, at 1.1821 trillion yen. Likewise, operating profit had been down 59% in the middle of the year, but by December the gap closed to 41%, at 296.7 billion yen.

In contrast to the previous term's net profits, which had been largely eroded by currency exchange losses, a weaker-than-anticipated yen improved net profits to 192.6 billion yen, down only 9% from the previous year. The year-end projections of 1.5 trillion yen in revenue, 370 billion yen of operating profit, and 230 billion of net profit are entirely achievable, and may even be exceeded.

The 2009 holiday season represents the second crucial event in Nintendo's recent history. Despite some stumbles, the company proclaimed loud and clear that their business continues to be a strong one, that their strength remains.

Having now covered the two most significant events in Nintendo's history since the publication of this book in Japanese in April 2009, I'd like to show that the conclusions drawn at the end of that edition remain valid.

It is undeniable that surprises from the company have been in short supply recently.

In the original epilogue, I wondered whether Nintendo would be able to continue to overcome its own limitations to bring smiles to the faces of consumers, and suggested that the company's greatest challenges lay before it.

Those challenges remain. Now as then, Iwata and Nintendo are in the midst of a new battle.

The DS was first released in the US in November 2004, with *Nintendogs* and *Brain Age*—the first salvos in the fight to increase the gaming population—hitting Japan in April and May 2005. After that came the US release of the Wii along with *Wii Sports* in November 2006, and *Wii Fit* in December 2007, titles which changed the idea of what home videogames could do.

The titles that have pulled the DS and Wii platforms behind them since then have been sequels or followups whose success is nearly guaranteed. 2009 saw the first major hit for the DS in some time in the form of *Dragon Quest IX*, the latest installment of the massively popular RPG series, practically guaranteed to sell well into the millions (it sold four million copies). All three of the major late 2009 hits for the Wii, too, were sequels to other successful titles.

Even as they struggle to create their next big surprise, Nintendo maintains the strength of their platforms by preparing sequels to already-popular games. It is a marvelous strategy, but soon we will begin to wonder when they will show us something new. Such questions are unavoidable; Nintendo has, after all, taught us to ask them.

There's no way to know whether that something new will be *Wii Relax*, or perhaps a new platform to follow up on the DS or the Wii. *Wii Relax* is only a single component of Nintendo's strategy of surprise, and there is no way to know whether it will be the hit Nintendo hopes it will be.

But we still believe that Nintendo will answer our hopes, and sooner rather than later—just like Apple did with the iPad tablet computer it announced in January 2010. And because Nintendo is— by its own reckoning—an entertainment and amusement company, we have higher hopes than even for Apple when it comes to gaming.

We'll be here, craning our necks, waiting for the next surprise.

Osamu Inoue
February 2010

The History of Nintendo

1889 Fusajiro Yamauchi, great-grandfather of Hiroshi Yamauchi (currently advisor), founds "Nintendo" at Ohashi Nishi-iru, Shomen-dori, Shimogyo Ward, Kyoto; begins manufacturing hanafuda playing cards
1902 First in Japan to manufacture Western-style playing cards
33 Partnership firm "Yamauchi Nintendo" set up
49 Hiroshi Yamauchi becomes third president at age 22

53 First in Japan to sell plastic playing cards

59 License with Walt Disney Company, launch of cards with Disney characters

62 Stocks listed at Osaka Securities Exchange 2nd Section and Kyoto Securities Exchange
63 Company name changed to "Nintendo Co., Ltd."

66 Launch of telescoping *Ultra Hand* based on Gunpei Yokoi's idea

70 Electronic toys *Ray Gun* and *Ray Gun SP* become a fad
77 Launch of Nintendo's first home gaming machine *TV Game 15*

80 Launch of *Game & Watch*; local corporation Nintendo of America Inc. (NOA) set up
81 Launch in U.S. of arcade game machine *Donkey Kong*

83/7 Launch of *Family Computer* (NES). Stocks listed at Tokyo Stock Exchange 1st Section

Stock price — Yen

80,000 / 70,000 / 60,000 / 50,000 / 40,000 / 30,000 / 20,000 / 10,000 / 0

1980 81 82 83 84

Operating Profit — Millions of Yen

600,000 / 500,000 / 400,000 / 300,000 / 200,000 / 100,000 / 0

Operating Profit / Sales

1981.8 82.8 83.8 84.3

Note: For periods ending August 1981 to August 1983, net income before taxes and other adjustments equals income before the same, and net income equals income. Period ending March 1990 settled in July due to accounting term change.

214

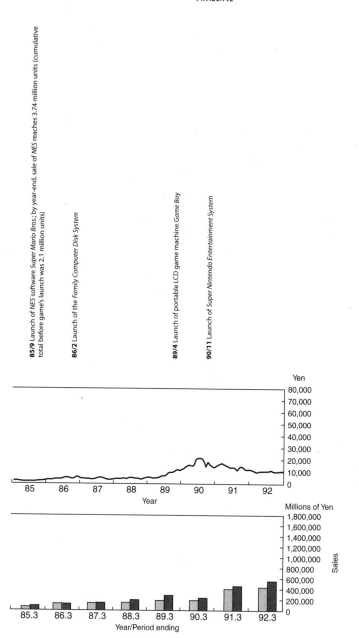

85/9 Launch of *NES* software *Super Mario Bros.*; by year-end, sale of *NES* reaches 3.74 million units (cumulative total before game's launch was 2.1 million units)

86/2 Launch of the *Family Computer Disk System*

89/4 Launch of portable LCD game machine *Game Boy*

90/11 Launch of *Super Nintendo Entertainment System*

Yen

80,000
70,000
60,000
50,000
40,000
30,000
20,000
10,000
0

85   86   87   88   89   90   91   92

Year

Millions of Yen

1,800,000
1,600,000
1,400,000
1,200,000
1,000,000
800,000
600,000
400,000
200,000
0

Sales

85.3   86.3   87.3   88.3   89.3   90.3   91.3   92.3

Year/Period ending

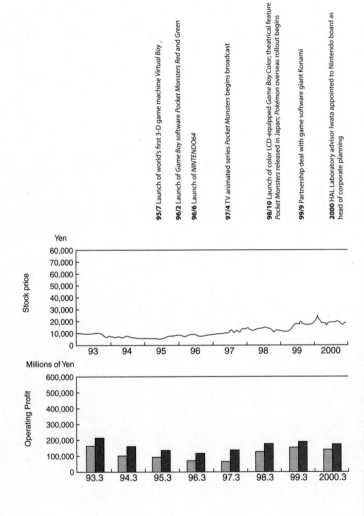

95/7 Launch of world's first 3-D game machine *Virtual Boy*

96/2 Launch of *Game Boy* software *Pocket Monsters Red and Green*

96/6 Launch of *NINTENDO64*

97/4 TV animated series *Pocket Monsters* begins broadcast

98/10 Launch of color LCD–equipped *Game Boy Color*; theatrical feature *Pocket Monsters* released in Japan; *Pokémon* overseas rollout begins

99/9 Partnership deal with game software giant Konami

2000 HAL Laboratory advisor Iwata appointed to Nintendo board as head of corporate planning

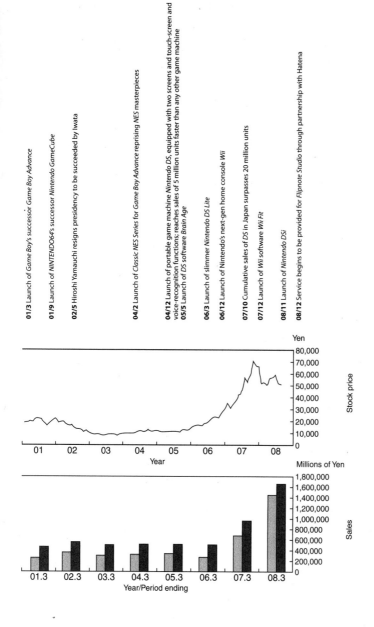

01/3 Launch of *Game Boy*'s successor *Game Boy Advance*

01/9 Launch of *NINTENDO64*'s successor *Nintendo GameCube*

02/5 Hiroshi Yamauchi resigns presidency to be succeeded by Iwata

04/2 Launch of *Classic NES Series* for *Game Boy Advance* reprising *NES* masterpieces

04/12 Launch of portable game machine *Nintendo DS*, equipped with two screens and touch-screen and voice-recognition functions; reaches sales of 5 million units faster than any other game machine
05/5 Launch of *DS* software *Brain Age*

06/3 Launch of slimmer *Nintendo DS Lite*

06/12 Launch of Nintendo's next-gen home console *Wii*

07/10 Cumulative sales of *DS* in Japan surpasses 20 million units

07/12 Launch of *Wii* software *Wii Fit*

08/11 Launch of *Nintendo DSi*

08/12 Service begins to be provided for *Flipnote Studio* through partnership with Hatena

Yen

Stock price

Year

Millions of Yen

Sales

Year/Period ending

Bibliography

In writing this book, the author consulted or quoted the following materials in addition to drawing from his own notes.

Newspapers

Nippon Keizai Shimbun

"Nintendo Shacho Yamauchi Hiroshi-shi—Asobi no Meijin 'Sofuto Inochi,' Gijutsu Dokusen de Ooatari (Toppu Kenkyu)," *Nikkei Sangyo Shimbun*. November 11, 1986.

"Nintendo Shacho Iwata Satoru-san (Furontorannaa)," *Asahi Shimbun*. June 19, 2004.

"Kyoto Sangyo Fudoki (1–5)," *Kyoto Shimbun*. April 7–May 12, 2000.

"Kyoto Sangyo Fudoki (18) Tabako-o to Tetsudo-o," *Kyoto Shimbun*. August 18, 2000.

"Tanba Furusato no Kimitachi E," *Kyoto Shimbun*. December 23, 2001.

"Make Way For The Q Wii N," *The People*. January 5, 2008.

"Keeping Up Nintendo's Momentum," *The Wall Street Journal*. August 4, 2008.

"Nintendo Makes More Profit Per Employee Than Goldman," *Financial Times*. September 15, 2008.

Magazines

"Famicom Kaihatsu Monogatari," *Nikkei Electronics*. January 31, 1994–September 11, 1995.

Jugemu. May 1995.

"Naze Watashi Wa Nintendo O Yameta Ka," *Bungei Shunju*. November 1996.

"Henshucho Intabyuu Iwata Satoru-shi Nintendo Shacho," *Nikkei Business*. October 17, 2005.

"Dai Ni Tokushu 'Okasan' o Nerae! Nintendo ga Wii ni Takusu Ocha no Ma Senryaku," *Nikkei Business*. November 27, 2006.

"Tokushu Nintendo wa Naze Tsuyoi 'Taka ga Goraku' no Sangyo Soshutsuryoku," *Nikkei Business*. December 17, 2007.

Books

Yokoi Gunpei Geemu Kan. Gunpei Yokoi with Makino Takefumi. Ascii.

Nintendo Shoho ni Himitsu: Ika Ni Shite "Kodomo Gokoro" wo Tsukanda ka. Kenji Takahashi. Shodensha.

Toranpu Monogatari. Michihiro Matsuda. Iwanami Shoten.

NHK Supesharu Shin Denshirikkoku 4 Bideo Geemu Kyofu no Kobo. Yutaka Aida and Atsushi Ogaki. Nippon Hoso Kyokai.

Otsuka Yakuho, vol. 513. Otsuka Seiyaku.

Web

"Kabunushi Toushika Muke no Joho." *Nintendo*.
http://www.nintendo.co.jp/ir/index.html

"Shacho ga Kiku Wii Purojekuto." *Nintendo*.
http://www.nintendo.co.jp/wii/topics/interview/vol1/index.html

"Shacho ni Manabe! Iwata Satoru-san." *Hobo Nikkan Itoi Shimbun*.
http://www.1101.com/president/iwata-index.html

"Ki no Ue no Himitsu Kichi." *Hobo Nikkan Itoi Shimbun*.
http://www.1101.com/nintendo/

"The World's Most Influential People," *Time*.
http://www.time.com/time/specials/2007/0,28757,1733748,00.html

"PC Watch, Goto Hiroshige no Weekly Kaigai Nyuusu, Nintendo Iwata Satoru Shacho Intabyuu (1)," *Impress*.
http://pc.watch.impress.co.jp/docs/2006/1206/kaigai324.htm

"Nikkei Business Online." *Nikkei BP Sha*.
http://business.nikkeibp.co.jp/

"ITpro." *Nikkei BP Sha*. http://itpro.nikkeibp.co.jp/

"nikkei TRENDYnet." *Nikkei BP Sha*. http://trendy.nikkeibp.co.jp/

"nikkei BPnet." *Nikkei BP Sha*. http://www.nikkeibp.co.jp/

The author furthermore wishes to express his deep appreciation for the assistance of the many people to whom he is indebted for the completion of this project, including Mr. Yoichi Wada, president of Square Enix; Mr. Masashi Morita, senior analyst at Okasan Securities; and Mr. Yoshihiro Taki, a former subordinate of Gunpei Yokoi.

ABOUT THE AUTHOR

Osamu Inoue was born in 1974 in Shizuoka Prefecture. After graduating from Keio University in 1999, he joined Nikkei Business Publications. As a reporter for *Nikkei Computer*, he wrote on IT currents and the web revolution. Transferred in 2004 to the flagship *Nikkei Business*, he experienced the auto, IT, and distribution beats. In 2009, after three years of investigative reporting on Nintendo, he was appointed staff writer for *Nikkei Business Online*.